THE ROYAL BABY BOOK

PHOEBE HICHENS

CRESCENT BOOKS
NEW YORK

John Scott, long-time friend of the Royal Family, has made a very special
contribution to this book. His pictures are relaxed and informal, like
those in a family album. Many shown here are little known. They give a
rare insight into the royal world – helping us to see, as never before, what
it's like to be born into this charmed circle.

*Edward VIII and George VI. This photograph
reminds one of the question, later addressed to the
little Princess Elizabeth: 'do you always drive in
bed?' (A team of toy horses was often to be found on
her eiderdown.)*

*More love of horses, this time from young Charles.
He used to cuddle his rocking horse like a live pet –
even pretending to feed it.*

First published in 1984
by Octopus Books Limited, 59 Grosvenor Street, London W1

Text © 1984 Phoebe Hichens
Layout and artwork © 1984 Conran Octopus Limited

Published 1984 by Crescent Books, distributed
by Crown Publishers Inc.

Library of Congress Cataloging in Publication Data
Hichens, Phoebe.
  The royal baby book.

  1. Great Britain—Princes and princesses—Biography.
2. Elizabeth II, Queen of Great Britain, 1926-   —
Family. 3. Windsor, House of. I. Title.
DA591.A1H53 1984 941.085'092'2 [B]   84-45564
ISBN 0-517-45466-1

Printed in Italy

Title page illustration

Prince William and his cousins Peter and Zara Phillips, with the
Princess of Wales.

Designed by Bob Hook and Ivor Claydon
Picture Research by Rosie Oxley

CONTENTS

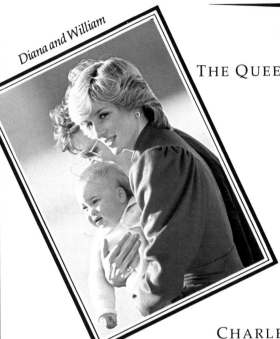

Diana and William

Prince William aged two

Charles and William

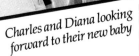

Charles and Diana looking
forward to their new baby

— INTRODUCTION —

oyal babies can be sure of at least two things. They will get a great deal of public attention. And they will be christened in great style, wearing a spectacular robe.

This robe was designed by Prince Albert, consort of Queen Victoria, for their first child. It is an extravagant concoction of white lace and satin, almost bridal-looking, and even reminiscent of the famous wedding dress worn by Diana, Princess of Wales.

'However hard you try,' Prince Philip once said, 'it's almost impossible to bring them up as ordinary children.' And he did try. He himself, as a Prince in exile, had been brought up the hard way, for there was no settled family home and little money. At times his clothes were patched, he had no raincoat, and it was only possible for him to buy a bicycle after long and careful hoarding of his pocket money.

Easy – no. Uncloistered and uninhibited – yes. And he would have liked his own children to enjoy some of the same freedom. But the fact is: the Royal Family wouldn't be 'royal' if it were ordinary, and ordinary freedom is something they can never take for granted. It's part of the pressure under which they must expect to live; and even the Queen Mother – a delightfully happy wife and mother – once exploded: 'We're not supposed to be human!'

Hundreds of years ago the pressures were different. Edward I took command of an army when he was in his early teens. Edward VI wrote more than a hundred essays in Latin before he was ten, and the young James I did three hours of Greek before breakfast. Nothing like that is expected of royal children today, but the out-of-the-ordinariness remains something the public expects.

Four generations: Edward VIII with father, George V; grandfather, Edward VII; and great grandmother, Victoria. Little Edward was a greater favourite with Victoria than any of her children and grandchildren had been. He climbed freely onto her lap and kissed her and called her Gan-Gan. When she died, he asked if there were Kings and Queens in Heaven. The answer was 'no, probably not'. Edward was rather amazed and persisted: 'Are you sure? No Kings and Queens at all?' The answer was still 'no'. At this, the little Prince shook his head and said: 'Gan-Gan won't like that!'

'I didn't suddenly sit up in my pram and think "yippee, I'm royal!"' Prince Charles once said. 'It all gradually dawned on me in rather a ghastly way.'

Ghastly? It seems an odd word. Can it really be 'ghastly' to grow up in a palace, with any number of toys and luxuries? to have the Queen as a mother? to expect, in due course, an income close to a million pounds a year?

Prince Charles would, of course, agree that royal children have massive privileges. (Young William, for example, has recently been given a miniature Jaguar valued at £60,000.) But members of the Royal Family do feel the pressure – 'the perfectly dreadful pressure' as Princess Margaret once called it – of the publicity.

It begins with the royal mother. The honeymoon is hardly over before the speculation begins. Is she . . . isn't she? And if not, *why not*? Princess Elizabeth said she fully expected to read the news of her pregnancy in the papers before she knew about it herself.

But then the good news. *She is*. And nowadays the palace announcement comes clean. No hiding behind the statement that Her Royal Highness will not be undertaking public engagements after such-and-such a date. Rather, Her Royal Highness will be expecting a baby in such-and-such a month. She's pregnant. But the pressure is still on. *Will everything be all right?* With improved medical care, a royal mother – like most women in the western world – can be pretty confident. And, unlike her forebears, she isn't expected to do ridiculous things such as wearing tight whalebone corsets all through her pregnancy. Even in the later stages, Mary Queen of Scots laced in her waist to twenty-two inches – the same measurements as Diana when she is *not* pregnant. Isabella of Castile, the first mother-in-law of Henry VIII, led her troops into battle one month before a baby was due.

Then the birth.

When the Queen Mother decided to have her second child in her home country, Scotland, there was consternation. Harry Boyd, Ceremonial Secretary to the Home Office, declared '. . . that some might think the *accouchement* was being conducted in an irregular hole-in-corner way'. He and the Home Secretary solemnly travelled north to be on hand when Princess Margaret Rose was born and bear witness that all was in order.

The baby Princess Elizabeth, with proud parents George VI and Elizabeth; her maternal grandparents, the Earl and Countess of Strathmore; and the royal grandparents, George V and Queen Mary. Comparing the faces of the two grandmothers, one can guess that a more indulgent attitude to royal children might be on the way – and it was. The mother, Elizabeth, had had a warm and loving childhood and was determined her own babies should have the same.

In family circles, this group were known as May, Bertie, Lilibet and Charlie. (Queen Mary had twelve names, but as she had been born in May, her mother added an unofficial nickname, calling her 'my may-flower'.) Trade union leader Joe Gormley once referred to the Prince of Wales by his family name of 'Charlie'. The Prince commented: 'It's better than being called Action Man.'

This pressure, at least, has been removed from the present Princess of Wales. But other pressures build up outside the Princess's hospital room.

The press are in full cry. Any photograph, any quote, any story, any scrap of information is hotly pursued. 'It's like being under seige,' a member of the Royal Household said. 'Reporters storming the battlements. Cameras trained like guns. It's a war of nerves.' It's also a tightrope operation. The defences must go up around the Princess and her baby; but the Royal Family cannot forget that part of their job is to be seen and heard – even hours after the baby is born. The press are a vital link between the Monarchy and the people, and some pictures, some information must be handed out. 'Nowadays,' Princess Alexandra once said, 'we have to compete with Elizabeth Taylor and the Beatles.' And even though the royal children are not expected to compete with Shirley Temple and other infant prodigies, they *are* exposed. They *are* expected to set an example.

The public, like Big Brother, are always watching and listening. And one of the first things the little Prince or Princess has to learn is that almost anything they do or say can make headlines in the world press. It's front-page news if Prince William sticks out his tongue at a photographer, if Princess Anne spanks her daughter, or if Prince Charles kisses his brother, Edward, continental-style, instead of pumping his hand British fashion. There are also pressures within the family. Any number of children know what it's like to be Number Two: to feel that the eldest brother or sister has special privileges because they came first. But the gap in the Royal Family – like so many other royal problems – is out of the ordinary. When you're second to a future King or Queen, the difference in pecking order is bound to be felt with extra sharpness.

In some cases there may have been more relief than envy. Young Prince George, later George V, came to love his naval career; and he was well aware that it would hardly be a career at all if he were Heir to the Throne. The elder brother, Eddy, was a welcome protection; and when he died, there was not only personal grief: the new Heir was dismayed by his loss of liberty.

But one is talking about the adult rather than the child. There may have been relief later on; but in early life the conditioning of the younger children to this strangely important

Prince Andrew holds younger brother Edward. Princess Anne cradles Andrew. An appearance of family affection among the young royals is important to the public – and it is genuine. But problems cropped up. Andrew, so much the youngest darling, was frankly jealous of the new darling. (Edward did indeed steal much favouritism.) Anne had to accept that a brother ten years younger than herself was second in line for the Throne – and she was now third.

Number One never came easily. Princess Margaret and Princess Anne were to find it difficult. And so, as the boy who grew up to be second in line to the Throne, did Prince Andrew.

Many other people live under pressure (and with great privileges, too). This is certainly true of Presidents, Prime Ministers and heads of big businesses. So what's all that different about the Royal Family? Probably the main royal difference is that it begins in the nursery – and goes on from there. (One comes back to Prince Philip's point that they just cannot be brought up as ordinary children.) And this has its advantages. When you are trained to do a special job pretty well from the word go, aren't you likely to do it better?

Mark Phillips admits that his first public engagements as a member of the Royal Family left him 'totally, totally shattered'. And he thinks that no one, unaccustomed to the role and all it expects, can have the least idea of the exhaustion involved. Shaking all those hands. Keeping on smiling. Finding things to say to endless strangers. At his first official lunch during their honeymoon . . . 'I sat between two ladies who couldn't speak a word of English. All we could do was draw little pictures and make sounds at each other.'

The in-built stamina of the royals never ceases to amaze those around them. On one Commonwealth tour, the Queen attended fifty parties, opened seven Parliaments, held a hundred and thirty-five receptions, made a hundred and fifty-seven speeches, listened to a further two hundred and seventy-six (with an appearance, at any rate, of polite interest), watched twenty-seven children's displays, laid seven wreaths, made four broadcasts and shook around thirteen thousand hands. When Princess Margaret went down with acute viral pneumonia on a tour of the South Pacific, she refused to be carried off the ship on a stretcher – even with a temperature of 105°. She told her secretary, Lord Napier: 'You will walk in front and the doctor will walk behind; and if I collapse, one of you will catch me.'

'They keep going when anyone else would give up,' commented a friend of the Queen's.

In America, the closest thing to a Royal Family is probably the Kennedy clan. Presidents come and go – and most of them soon cease to be a focus of interest. But the Kennedys, like the British royals, remain in a glare of publicity. Whatever they do, whatever they say, it's news; and when John-John went to school, one of the masters said: 'I think it was like Prince Charles going to Cheam. Reporters and photographers were around the whole time. The pressure on him and on us was terrific.'

It was something which David, the tragic son of Robert Kennedy, talked about. He said the pressure never let up. He couldn't cope with it. Other members of his family found it close to unbearable.

The British Royal Family make mistakes, throw up misfits. But all in all, they *do* seem able to cope. The number of suicides, drug addicts, alcoholics or rebels is surprisingly low. And maybe it's the long tradition, together with the early start, which makes the difference. It all happened quite suddenly to the Kennedys. But as an American once said: 'The British royals aren't exactly brilliant. You just feel they've been *at it* for so long.'

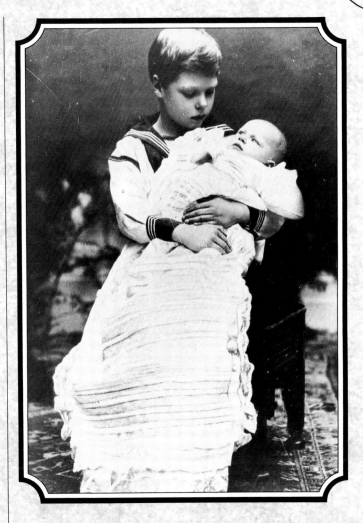

There is something rather sad about this photograph if one remembers the future of these two children. The elder, Edward VIII, was to become an exile from his home country. His was, in many ways, to be a frustrated life. The baby George, Duke of Kent – handsomest of the brothers – was to be killed at the age of forty.

THE QUEEN MOTHER AND HER DAUGHTERS

The Queen and her daughters: Elizabeth aged eight and a half and Margaret Rose aged four and a half.

It is tempting to say the Queen Mother transformed family life for the young royals. Tempting, but not quite true. Certainly there was a contrast between the life of her little daughters and the atmosphere in which the children of George V had been raised. Queen Mary was caring but shy. Hugging and kissing was never the order of the day; and even as a grandmother, she was forbidding. But George V's mother, Alexandra, was quite the opposite: a doting, demonstrative mother – so inclined to spoil her darlings that Queen Victoria called them 'ill bred and ill trained'. Queen Elizabeth achieved something more complete. She was loving, but not over-possessive or over-indulgent. There was a closeness in the family unit – not possible with a husband like Edward VII – so the little Princesses felt there was love all round. Love between husband and wife as well as between parents and children.

The girls were not brought up in an extravagant style. The food was good but simple and they were encouraged to grow vegetables in their own gardens. It was early to bed, with an apple; and only a shilling a week for pocket money. Part of this shilling had to be saved for Christmas shopping which often took place at Woolworth's. Listing the presents given to her, Elizabeth includes three pony books, a box of chocolate peppermints, a tin of toffees, and a lovely bookmark and calendar. Margaret was given a seesaw and dolls with dresses by her mother, an umbrella from Papa, and a pen and pencil from one of the Equerries. Their governess felt the gifts erred on the side of economy.

The relationship between the two sisters was, in some ways, very normal. 'Wait for me, Lilibet, wait for me!' The signature tune of many sisters four years younger. 'Margaret always wants what *I* want.' 'Elizabeth would pinch and I would kick. I never won.' But when their father became King, the gap between the Heir and the second daughter widened. There was no loss of love. Margaret just had to accept a difference in privilege.

Not all the Heir's privileges were enviable. When Elizabeth went off to take lessons in constitutional history with the Provost of Eton, Margaret may have been happy to stay behind. But she did feel excluded from the special sessions between the elder sister and beloved Papa. How could she help noticing that it was Elizabeth who took the salute at a rehearsal for the Aldershot Tattoo? Elizabeth who was made Colonel of the Grenadier Guards at the age of fifteen? Elizabeth who, two years later, was made Councillor of State while the King was abroad and required to sign important papers? (One of them was a reprieve for a murderer.) 'I was born too late!' the younger sister once exclaimed.

There can be no doubt that the Queen Mother managed to ease the problems – because it was so evident she loved them both. So, too, did the King – who was even accused of favouring Margaret. He laughed at her antics and mimicry. He forgave her impertinence. Nothing delighted him more than when she climbed on his knee and demanded 'windy water' (her name for soda water).

To this day the bond between the two sisters remains very close. And when the younger was asked what she felt to be her most important job in life, she replied simply: 'To back up the Queen.'

It was still possible in those days for the Royal Family to walk around – in a railway station, for instance – without attracting crowds and photographers. It is unlikely that Charles and Diana and children could do the same.

The two babies, Elizabeth and Margaret Rose, were real look-alikes. And the physical resemblance was increased by their mother's habit of dressing them in nearly identical clothes. But they were to grow up as two very different personalities – the elder, so careful and conscientous, the younger, bubbling, funny, greedy, wilful and enchanting.

Elizabeth was fourteen when she made her first broadcast. It was during the war. 'All we children at home are full of cheerfulness and courage . . . we know in the end all will be well.' She concluded: 'Come on, Margaret!' And Margaret chimed in to say goodnight.

When the little Princesses were enrolled in the Guides by the Princess Royal, Elizabeth wrote, 'We were all terribly nervous . . . but when Aunt Mary came in, we could see she was nervous also. Then we felt quite at home.'

ELIZABETH AND PHILIP

What would have happened if the eighteen-year-old sea cadet had *not* been a Prince? If the thirteen-year-old Princess had fallen in love, at first sight, with the son of Mr and Mrs X from Birmingham?

The answer – probably – is unromantic. They would never have been married.

Even more realistically, they might never even have met. When King George and his family visited the naval college at Dartmouth in 1939, young Philip was chosen to look after the Princesses, not because he was blond and blue-eyed and handsome, but because he was the nephew of Lord Louis Mountbatten, the King's naval aide-de-camp.

There were other connections, too, with the British Royal Family. He was a descendant of Queen Victoria. And his father, Prince Andrew of Greece, had been rescued from possible execution at the hands of a revolutionary junta by the direct intervention of George V. Philip had no riches, no kingdom; but he belonged in the royal circle. He could expect invitations to Buckingham Palace or Windsor Castle.

As a commoner he could – like Peter Townsend – have become a member of the Royal Household and fallen in love with the boss's daughter. But Philip loved the sea and would, almost certainly, have pursued a naval career. Without royal connections, he could not have expected to make contact with a future Queen.

Royal marriages have long been a matter of suitability. Victoria and Albert drew up lists of possible wives for their eldest son, Edward, and sent his sister to inspect the favourite candidate. Princess Vicky reported on Princess Alexandra almost as one might on a pedigree animal. 'Lovely figure but very thin' . . . 'regular teeth' . . . 'prettily marked eyebrows' . . . 'forehead well shaped and not at all flat' . . . 'well-shaped nose but a little long'.

Princess May of Teck was more or less 'chosen' for the bridegroom; and George V allowed that he 'was not particularly in love' when he proposed. The love came later; and in spite of his infidelities, the same was true of Edward VII. 'He loved me best,' his wife maintained.

The romance of Elizabeth and Philip did not – like the romance of Edward VIII and Mrs Simpson – mark a dramatic departure from royal tradition. He belonged in the family. There were no previous wives, or even scandals. He was a fine, upstanding young man with a splendid war record. What objections could there be,

particularly as they were so obviously in love?

But objections there were. The King looked suspicious. He counselled delay. His daughter was too young, too inexperienced. He insisted on separating them for four months when Elizabeth accompanied him on a tour of South Africa. Why?

For once, it was not an out-of-the-ordinary, royal problem. It was one shared by innumerable fathers who, quite simply, dread the idea of losing a beloved daughter. Of course she would have to marry sometime – but not yet. It was a question of finding excuses rather than giving valid reasons; and when, after her wedding, he wrote to her '. . . I felt I had lost something very precious' . . . this summed it all up.

The opposition of her father was one problem. And there were aspects of the courtship which, to a young and essentially shy girl, had to be painful. Before Philip had even proposed, there were headlines in the popular press: 'SHOULD OUR QUEEN WED PHILIP?' She came back from visiting a factory in tears. 'It was horrible. They all shouted at me "Where's Philip?" '

But the Queen would never deny that luck was massively on her side. She fell in love with the right man and he with her. And the November wedding in 1947 has always been described as the best possible tonic for a grey Britain where people still counted their clothing coupons and eked out their butter rations.

Twenty-five years later, the Queen was to tell the story of the Bishop who, when asked what he thought about sin, replied succinctly: 'I'm against it.' If asked what she thought about marriage, her reply would be equally concise. 'I'm for it.'

When Elizabeth heard that Lieutenant Philip Mountbatten was coming to see her act as Prince Charming in the pantomime at Windsor, it's said she lit up like a Christmas tree. It's also said that her radiance had its effect: this was when Philip began to fall seriously in love. Although shy and reserved, Elizabeth had never been able to hide her feelings. The look she gives him in this photograph (right) says it all.

Young Philip, left, at Gordonstoun, dressed for his part in the school production of Macbeth. *(He had a lot of hair in those days.)*

PRINCE CHARLES

BORN 4 NOVEMBER 1948, UNDER THE SIGN OF SCORPIO

ost parents are delighted with a new-born Scorpio. He looks rounded, 'finished', good tempered. But they grow up to be tougher than appearances suggest: ambitious, sometimes ruthless, restless, interested in world affairs. (More American Presidents are born under this sign than any other.) They are often religious. (Billy Graham is a Scorpio.) And with great sex appeal. (So was Grace Kelly.) Varicose veins and accidents in sports are common. They make a good boss, but employees – and wives – have to be careful because of this tougher-than-they-look aspect. The motto of another Scorpio, Theodore Roosevelt, was: 'Speak softly, but carry a big stick.'

Princess Elizabeth made no secret of her desire to have a son as soon as possible. A male heir has always been important in a royal family; and in medieval Italy streets were draped in black flags when a Princess arrived, indicating public disappointment.

Word got around on the morning of 4 November that the birth was imminent, and crowds gathered around Buckingham Palace. Excitement surged when at last a page ran out and whispered in the ear of a police inspector. Turning round, the officer bellowed through cupped hands: 'It's a Prince!' The great throng exploded into cheers and songs; and the uproar was such, a palace official had to make a further announcement: could they please quieten down because they were keeping the Queen awake? (They did.)

A large sunny room, once used as a schoolroom for the little Princesses, had been turned into a nursery. But there had been no great outlay on baby equipment. Charles's cot was a miniature four-poster, brought down from the attics and about four hundred years old. His pram had been used by his mother and Aunt Margaret. (It was large and cumbersome.) Even his first toy, an ivory-handled rattle, had been rattled by earlier royals.

So it was that Charles Arthur Philip George – the boy who was to become His Royal Highness the Prince of Wales, Earl of Chester, Duke of Cornwall, Duke of Rothesay, Earl of Carrick, Baron Renfrew, Lord of the Isles, Great Steward of Scotland and Knight of the Garter – so it was that he began life.

'He was the eldest. He always had a great sense of responsibility,' Rose Kennedy said. She was talking about her own son, Joe, a shining young man, by all accounts, who was killed in the war. His family expected him to be President of the United States.

The baby Charles, born 14 November 1948, was luckier than many earlier Princes of Wales. He would not be obliged to marry a 'she-wolf' princess from France, like Edward II. He would not be cordially disliked by both parents, like 'poor Fred', son of George II. Unlike Edward VII, he would not – aged seven and a half – have to spend six hours in the schoolroom learning religion, English, writing, French, music, calculating, German, drawing and geography. Charles was to have problems. But not these.

Prince Arthur, seventh child of Victoria. One suspects he would not have been allowed to beat his drum with such vigour, even though Albert loved to play games with his children – flying kites, chasing butterflies, turning somersaults on a haystack.

During this photographic session, Charles – when he had finished beating his drum – hid in a sentry box and wouldn't come out. Photographer John Scott said: 'He'd better stay there until we finish the chocolates.' Charles heard – and was out in a trice.

One notices that earlier royal parents dressed their baby sons (seen here, Edward VIII and George VI) to look like baby girls. Young Charles, on the other hand, is very much the little boy. So, from a very early age, was Prince William. The present Prince and Princess of Wales might disapprove, too, of the dummy in George's mouth. Their babies are certainly not allowed one.

The Queen Mother chose a Scottish governess for her daughters. And the preference for Scottish 'minders' continued. Nurse Lightbody, seen here with Charles, was a Scot. The Northern influence carried through to the under-nanny, Mabel Anderson, who came from Lancashire.

Charles, too, has had from a very early age a great sense of responsibility. And the pressures came, in rather different ways, from both parents. On the one hand, there was his mother. In private life, she has an enchanting sense of humour; but her attitude to the Monarchy is serious and dedicated. She expected the same from her eldest son.

Prince Philip, like many fathers, wanted a son who followed in his own footsteps. He was a natural athlete and a great believer in tough, physical education; and the lessons in dancing, deportment and piano playing, arranged for the small Charles, hardly met with his approval. He favoured football matches and work-outs in the gym.

Charles found the expectations of both parents pretty hard. He was shy, easily given to tears, ready to shrink from too much public attention. His first governess, Katherine Peebles, remembers him as 'rather a nervous child'; and the tough-guy sports pushed by his father did not always appeal. None of this was made easier when the decision was taken to send him to school.

It was the first time this had happened to the Heir to the Throne. And although the secluded schoolroom for royal brothers and sisters was obviously out of date, the immediate effect on a shy, 'slightly nervous' boy was devastating. His prep school, Cheam, was besieged by

reporters and photographers, and no less than sixty-eight stories about him were published in his first eighty-eight days. Schoolfellows were bribed to steal his exercise books, report on his essays and relate any anecdote, however trivial. (Not a good climate for making friends.)

Charles the chubby toddler soon became the small boy who loved trains and particularly enjoyed talking to the engine driver. Later he appreciated the story of his grandfather, George VI, who presented the O.B.E. to the driver of the royal train, not at Buckingham Palace, but on the platform of Euston station, as a surprise!

Photographer John Scott remembers Charles saying virtuously: 'We must tidy up the garden before Mummy comes home.'

It's an idyllic family group. But did the elder brother – like so many elder brothers – play boss to the little sister? Judging by the determined, not altogether sweet-tempered look on her face, one suspects she knew how to stand up for herself. And by all accounts, that's just what she did. It's said, too, that Charles was a very affectionate little boy – sometimes to excess. During a photographic session with the baby Anne, he was asked to kiss her. He obeyed with such squeezing enthusiasm that she burst into tears.

Even the robust Prince Philip began to wonder if the experiment could work. The press were told that, unless the harassment ceased, the boy would have to leave. It would be back to the royal schoolroom. And the message went home. The publicity died down and life became more tolerable.

But Charles was never really happy, either at Cheam or his next school, Gordonstoun. Everything would have been easier if, like his younger brother Andrew, he had been more of a natural athlete and a boisterous extrovert. As it was, he relied more than anything on his determination. If he were not to disappoint his father, he must be good at sports; and he did indeed become a good footballer, swimmer, skier – and an outstandingly good polo player. If he were not to disappoint his mother, he must get over the shyness and learn to cope with people, public speaking and publicity in general.

Two things helped him. One was a natural talent for acting, which runs in the Royal Family. (Not so much inherited by his mother, but very much by his Aunt Margaret.) If you can come on stage and play Macbeth, as he did at Gordonstoun; or switch to comedy roles, as he did at Cambridge, and act a cello-playing pop star ('the best plucker in the business') or a Victorian lecher or a caricature of a weather forecaster in gas mask and frogman's flippers – obviously this helps you to get over

The Royal Family are pretty good fanatics about fresh air and exercise. We don't know if the Queen goes jogging before breakfast round the gardens of Buckingham Palace or if Prince Philip works out in some private gym. But the number of photographs showing the royals involved in some sport tells

the story. Hunting, polo, skiing, shooting, cricketing, swimming, sailing, surfing, racing, carriage racing – they all have the royal seal of approval. So do good healthy walks through the heather, with picnics in the rain. Very definitely, the pressure was on young Charles to fall in line.

public appearance nerves.

Another help was his two terms at Timbertop, Australia. For the first time in his life, he felt everyone around him was relaxed and not too impressed by his royal background. 'I was just one of the boys,' he said. 'It was such a relief.'

The older Charles still comes across as gentle, concerned, a little diffident. There are undertones of: 'why has all this happened to *me*?' But the determination to make a success of his role is there. And the Scorpio assessment that he is 'tougher than he looks' is probably right.

Left to himself, one wonders if the Prince would have been as 'sporty' as these photographs suggest. The 'slightly nervous' child, who was cautious with ponies and quivered at the deep end of the swimming pool, might well have been happier to be left indoors, playing his cello or his favourite records and planning the next game of charades. But a friend of his once said: 'He's not unusually talented, but he's so determined. If he decides to be good at sport, he'll succeed – and even come to enjoy it.'

PRINCESS ANNE

Leo is the sign of the lion. And although Leos can show quick rage – particularly if they feel someone is poaching on their territory and showing too much familiarity – the roar is often worse than the bite. There is arrogance and no man can expect a Leo girl to worship at his feet; but she likes people who stand up to her and never respects a pushover. There's a strong sense of responsibility for the weak and helpless. She likes tailored clothes and fine materials, but definitely not frills and ruffles. She is very protective of her children but stands no nonsense if she thinks they're at fault. Princess Anne shares the sign with Napoleon Bonaparte, Alfred Hitchcock and – perhaps unexpectedly – Mae West.

When Princess Elizabeth became pregnant for the second time, she was busy making a home of Clarence House. There was a lot of modernizing to be done, and even the nursery was not finished on time. For the first few months of her life, the baby Anne slept in her father's dressing room.

Charles was an affectionate little boy and seemed delighted with his sister. 'Come and see the new baby,' he would say, tugging at the hands of visitors. In the early years he was protective, though sometimes scolding. 'You're such a *trouble* to me,' he declared when Anne misbehaved.

There were to be more troubles later on. Anne did not take meekly to Number Two place in the family; and one of her first memories is total fury when elder brother was swept off to Westminster Abbey to attend the Coronation of their mother – and she was left behind. There was even greater rage when, a few years later, Khrushchev and Bulganin visited Britain and presented Charles with a most desirable pony. She was palmed off with a bear, and what was the use of that? It had to go straight to the zoo.

Anne in Gibraltar. She went round busily, feeding peanuts to the apes. No fear of animals in her case, though it's reported that brother Charles hung back. When, however, an ape attempted to take the whole bag, Anne's gesture said plainer than words: 'Oh no you don't!' Even as a baby, the little Princess was adventurous. She never hid behind Mummy's skirts or clung, anxiously, to nanny's hand. She'd be crawling or toddling off on her own to see what the flower beds, or any other part of the world, had to offer. And she adored playing all sorts of games. Perhaps this is why under-nanny Mabel Anderson admitted that Anne was her favourite.

You might not think the knitted jacket, worn here by Anne, should set the fashion world buzzing. But it was like the time when their mother, as a little girl, appeared in a yellow frock — and yellow became the 'in' colour far and wide. These jackets became the jackets for the young.

Unlike her own children, Princess Anne was to have traditional royal names: Anne Elizabeth Alice Louise.

It's possible that Anne's competitive, sometimes aggressive nature was sharpened by this sense of coming second. She was out to prove that, in some areas at least, she would come first; and with a brother like Charles, this wasn't always difficult. Anne had inherited much of her father's toughness and fearlessness and there was the family flair for riding. Putting the two together, she soon proved herself the better on horseback. She fell off, inevitably, but never seemed to mind – not even when she was once literally whipped from the saddle by an unseen washing line strung out across her path.

Charles was unhappy at school. Anne took it in her stride (bolstered by the fact that her beloved pony, High Jinks, was allowed to come too). She settled down at Benenden in Kent with few traumas, played tennis and lacrosse enthusiastically, was not too worried when she proved a bit of a dunce at maths, perhaps remembering that her mother had had the same problem and that the Queen Mother simply said: 'maths don't matter.'

Her affection for her old school was demonstrated recently on the occasion of their Diamond Jubilee. Anne attended, and insisted on going ahead with a tree-planting ceremony even though it was a dreadful, drenching December day. More revealingly, she said in her speech: 'I'm very happy to be back home.'

As she grew older, Anne began to see the advantages of *not* being Heir to the Throne. Number Two had its compensations. The unfailing politeness, the uncontroversial comments expected of her elder brother were not so essential in her case. It might not make a good impression when she snapped at an American reporter: 'I'm not your love. I'm Your Royal Highness.' Nor when, asked of her reactions to the birth of Prince William, she came back: 'That's my business, thank you very much.' But she was not likely to be a future Monarch, and speaking her own mind seemed a privilege to which she was entitled.

How many times have you seen Princess Anne giving or receiving prizes at some horsey event? This is one of the earliest occasions, in 1960, when she was to award a rosette as part of her public engagements.

This did not mean, however, that all royal responsibilities could be shrugged off. (Only some of the frills.) She takes seriously the chores – even if it means presenting leeks to the men of the Welsh Guards on St David's day or naming a hovercraft. It was more congenial when she visited the 14th/20th Hussars in Germany as their Colonel-in-Chief, drove a Chieftain tank and fired a submachine gun from the hip. But her work for Save the Children has been gruelling and painful. She has travelled into the heart of the African bush with temperatures well over 100°. She has visited leper colonies and tragic areas where one child in every two is going to die. She is almost afraid to express her feelings about these children. She says that if she thought too much about each individual tragedy, 'I would just go nuts.'

Could be that she's the opposite of Charles. Not as tough as she looks.

Looking through the photographs of Anne growing up, it all looks very normal. There she is as a Brownie. There she is with her pony (High Jinks). There she is in a fairly unnoticeable blue coat. The Queen was indeed economy-minded about children's clothes (like Victoria who favoured kilts because they could be passed on to younger boys **and** girls). It's a pity we don't have a picture of the dramatic incident when Anne tried to lead her pony up the steps of Sandringham and ride him into the drawing room to surprise her parents.

A little-known fact about Anne is that she loved being photographed in pretty dresses like this one. On one occasion she flirted so outrageously with the camera, the Queen told the photographer: 'Don't encourage her — she'll want to be a filmstar.'

— PRINCE ANDREW —

BORN 17 FEBRUARY 1960, UNDER THE SIGN OF AQUARIUS

Aquarius is a sign which includes many filmstars – like Clark Gable, Paul Newman, Tallulah Bankhead and Vanessa Redgrave. (Though, on the intellectual side, one has to reckon with Charles Darwin and Galileo.) They tend to be unconventional, sometimes flamboyant in youth, but must watch out for creeping lethargy and hardening of the arteries as they grow older. Interests are widespread: cricket, cars, pictures, astronauts, alcoholism, medical discoveries or a fantastic new recipe for sausages . . . they can be intrigued by almost anything. They seek quantity rather than quality in their relationships with other people and girlfriends should watch out: Aquarians are not good at 'going steady'. They tend to like the woman who is a bit of a mystery, who they can't figure out.

At this age Andrew was a special favourite, not only with his parents but also with the Palace staff. Below stairs he was known as Andy Pandy – after a popular puppet on children's television.

The 'is she . . . isn't she?' pressures were beginning to die down. Nine years after the birth of Princess Anne, the public concluded that the Queen thought two was enough. The announcement that a third was on the way came as quite a shock.

The Queen became pregnant at an awkward moment. She was due to embark on a nine-week tour of Canada plus a visit to Ghana; and although the whole programme could not be carried out, Elizabeth was determined to do as much as possible. Off they went to Canada with a dressmaker, specially skilled in discreet 'letting out' of royal outfits, in attendance.

It's ironic that the most extrovert of the royal children – the one who really seems to enjoy publicity – should have been far more protected than his elder sister and brother. The Queen and Prince Philip had not wanted too much exposure for Charles and Anne, but they accepted that some was unavoidable. Enter young Andrew and it was decided that he should be brought up as quietly and privately as possible. There was so little exposure that rumours circulated that 'something was wrong'. Might he be deformed? a mongol? deaf and dumb?

The crowds outside Buckingham Palace always hope a royal head might peep out of a window. Did they see this long shot of Prince Andrew? Not likely. The Palace nurseries face over the gardens.

Andrew displays, aged six, his love of travelling and adventure.

This is the London playground of the royals, young and old. Behind high spiked walls are thirty-nine acres of garden, complete with lake. Albert fell in once while skating. So did the young Elizabeth while bird-watching. No dramas here with Andrew and Edward as they play with the corgis. Although the Queen is liable to appear and say, 'Don't tease the dogs!'

In due course, the appearance of an exceptionally sturdy, impish, talkative young fellow made nonsense of the rumours. It also became clear that he was the naughtiest of the Royal Family.

The royals have long been fond of practical jokes. The middle-aged Edward VII encourged apple pie beds at house parties in Sandringham. Prince Charles pressed a sticky, sucked sweet into his mother's gloved hand just before she was due to greet some dignitary. But Andrew outdid them all. There was bubble bath in the royal swimming pool at Windsor. He would tie together the bootlaces of the palace sentries as they stood on duty. (They were not allowed to move and a sergeant would have to come and disentangle them.) A priceless silver tray vanished at Buckingham Palace: Andrew had secreted it to use as a toboggan up and down a wide staircase.

At ten years old, it was clear that Andrew was going to be very handsome.

'It was always hard to get Prince Andrew to stand still,' photographer John Scott recalls. 'It took a lot of persuasion to get him posing, so quiet and good, beside this chair; and you couldn't count on it lasting more than a few minutes.'

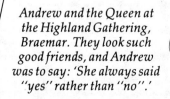

Andrew and the Queen at the Highland Gathering, Braemar. They look such good friends, and Andrew was to say: 'She always said "yes" rather than "no".'

24

The greatest confusion occurred during a Buckingham Palace garden party. Someone (and everyone thought it was Andrew) turned the signs around. The ladies went in to powder their noses in the gents. The gents were directed to the kitchens. Guests were advised to leave their coats in the Queen's private apartments. And so it went on, with hapless palace officials trying to get things back under control. 'He's not always a little ray of sunshine,' commented the Queen.

Andrew supplanted his sister Anne as the second Heir to the Throne. And once again there was a sense of rivalry, a special need to assert himself. The childhood pranks may have been one sign, his bossiness at school another. Schoolfellows remember him as a bit of a bully –

and very inclined to remind them that he was the son of the Queen. It was also noticed that he was proud of growing taller and handsomer than his brother. 'He's the one with the Robert Redford looks,' commented Prince Charles, with a touch of sourness. And the filmstar quality of Prince Andrew has its drawbacks.

Aquarians, like Clark Gable, feel they belong centre stage. (So did Franklin D. Roosevelt.) Princess Anne could concentrate on being exceptionally brilliant at one thing – riding; but Prince Andrew, with a more general sense of showmanship, finds it hard to settle down. He can return, as a war hero, from the Falklands and that's fine. But in the long run, what is he to do? what is he to be?

The question has still to be answered.

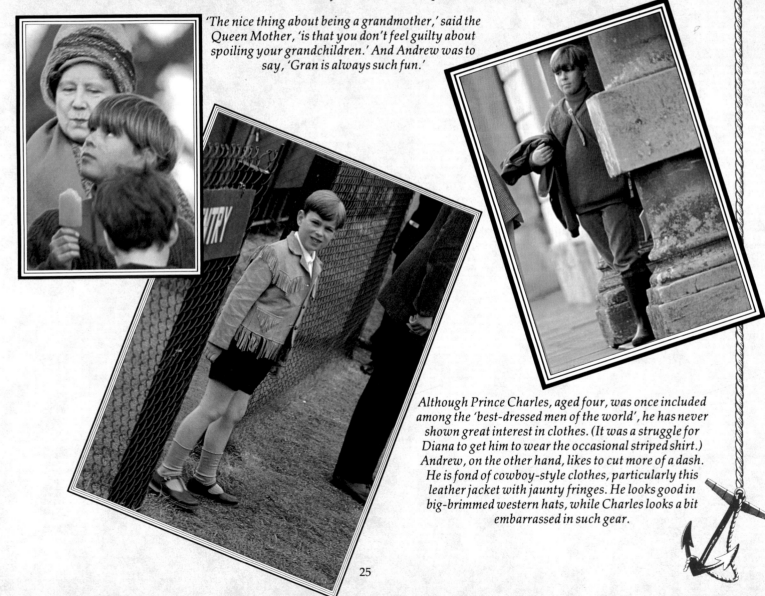

'The nice thing about being a grandmother,' said the Queen Mother, 'is that you don't feel guilty about spoiling your grandchildren.' And Andrew was to say, 'Gran is always such fun.'

Although Prince Charles, aged four, was once included among the 'best-dressed men of the world', he has never shown great interest in clothes. (It was a struggle for Diana to get him to wear the occasional striped shirt.) Andrew, on the other hand, likes to cut more of a dash. He is fond of cowboy-style clothes, particularly this leather jacket with jaunty fringes. He looks good in big-brimmed western hats, while Charles looks a bit embarrassed in such gear.

PRINCE EDWARD

*Edward was the fourth child, but the crowds showed the same enthusiasm
for him as a baby as they had done for Charles.*

he typical Pisces is not a fighter. His instinct, like an easy-going fish, is to swim with the current. There will be times when he struggles against this let-it-all-glide approach; but he does not thrive on opposition. His vitality depends on doing his own thing – not swimming upstream. Physically, he can be remarkably gifted and graceful. (Like Nijinsky and Nureyev.) He can also be creative. (Like Chopin, Handel and Michelangelo.) Given the right to follow his own talents, he can work hard. But burning ambition is not part of his make-up. He tends to be dreamy, romantic, sometimes melancholic, no great handyman and no great money-maker. He needs to marry a very sensible heiress.

It's possible that the youngest Prince had the happiest upbringing of all four children. He was an appealing, gentle child. 'Quite the quietest,' said his mother. And on another occasion: 'it isn't fair a boy should have such long eyelashes.'

He had no desire to rival or 'prove himself' against the elder brothers and sister; and the passionate public interest – sharpened by the unexpected advent of Andrew – did not extend so obtrusively to him. He was allowed to be sheltered and private and, until quite recently, could have walked in the park or down a London street without anyone recognizing him.

Probably he was the one child the Queen could just relax and enjoy. Her accession to the Throne happened when Charles and Anne were still very young and she was bound to be a very busy, preoccupied mother. There was more time for Andrew; but he was a bit of a handful and, when the younger brother came along, his nose was put out of joint quite considerably. At the time he was four years old and very aware that a lot of parental love and attention was going elsewhere.

Edward may have had to endure teasing, even bullying from brother Andrew. On the other hand, he was adored and indulged by Charles. His father still expected a son to be good at sports and Edward learned to swim, ride, play football and cricket. (Swimming lessons were supervised by Prince Philip himself in the pool at Buckingham Palace.) But the pressure was off. At Balmoral, if Edward wanted to stay quietly at home with a book instead of tramping the moors, shooting, fishing and picnicking in the rain – that's just what he did.

If the Queen was depressed, it was Edward who could coax her out of it. 'You're such a pretty girl,' he used to say. 'Such a pretty, pretty girl.' And the smiles would be back.

His happy childhood owed much to the daughter of a policeman from Lancashire. Mabel Anderson was twenty-two when she advertised her services as a nanny in *The Lady* magazine. The summons for an interview, first at St James's, then at Buckingham Palace, came as a shock to the quiet, soft-spoken girl. Even more amazing: she was offered the job of looking after the baby son of Princess Elizabeth and Prince Philip.

Edward didn't like being left behind on the yacht Britannia while his mother went ashore. (This time on a visit to Norway.) But one of the sailors became his 'minder' and soon distracted the little Prince.

Another idyllic family picture. But, perhaps more than any other of the royal children, Andrew was to feel that 'someone is sitting in my place'. No question of his being supplanted as second in line for the Throne; just the niggle felt by so many children: 'am I coming second in attention?'

Here it looks as if the young Prince, proudly holding the cup, has just won the carriage race himself at Windsor Great Park. In fact, the champion was the Crown Equerry.

So Mabel began with Charles and went on to Edward. She was under-nanny to Nurse Lightbody, who ruled the nursery roost; but Mabel's genius was for playing with children, for helping them to have fun. Prince Philip might drill them in the swimming pool or on the cricket pitch. The Queen snatched time to give them their baths and read aloud from favourite books. But it was Mabel who played hopscotch on the palace terrace, who helped with their baby pictures and stuck them up on the nursery walls, who painted their faces and played Red Indians, who invented mad and magical stories about fairies and monsters.

Once again, Edward – the last darling – came in for the fun rather than the pressure, the discipline. And there was another bonus. An influx of royal cousins, close to his own age, made for a more sociable childhood. The little Princesses, Elizabeth and Margaret, had been close to isolation. A special troop of Girl Guides was formed to give them some get-together with other children. But they *were* children from 'outside'. It was not the same as socializing with members of the same family, without fear of fingers pointing – 'he's royal, he's different'.

Like the other children of the Queen, Edward went to school. He followed Andrew to Heatherdown, a prep school close to Windsor, and then to Gordonstoun. (Again, he was lucky: the Spartan regime, still prevailing at Gordonstoun when Charles arrived, had been relaxed. There were no wintry runs before breakfast and the swimming pool was actually heated.) He did reasonably well at everything, but without covering himself with glory.

The young Prince remains something of an enigma. He does not have the abrasiveness of his sister, Anne, but he dislikes publicity. 'Please go away and photograph something interesting, which I'm not,' he has told reporters. When asked to pose at Wanganui Collegiate School in New Zealand, where he had been engaged as a teacher, he said: 'Do you mind? I'm here to earn a living.'

He tries. And for him, more than most, it means swimming upstream in order to fill the bill of a royal Prince. But perhaps, like the talented stars born under his sign (they include, incidentally, his uncle by marriage, Tony Armstrong Jones), he should be allowed to explore his own talents and swim along with them.

Full Highland dress can be vastly becoming, as illustrated by Andrew, Edward and their grandfather, George VI. But not all royals have carried it off so well. The first British King to wear Highland dress was George IV – such a corpulent figure, it was hard to make a kilt big enough. Nor do kilts make fat people look any slimmer. As George observed his reflection, with the huge pleats and the flesh-coloured tights, he commented: 'I cannot help smiling at myself.'

A special relationship. Sarah Armstrong Jones has always been very close to the Queen; and Sarah and Edward have grown up together, almost like twins. She is still his favourite dancing partner or companion to the theatre.

The Queen was anxious to give Edward as private and as normal an upbringing as possible. But the time came for him to take on public engagements. Here he is at Windsor, undertaking the first.

The youngest Prince was not nearly as active and boisterous as Andrew. It was unusual to find him running around, as here. It was more characteristic of him to sit quietly with a book.

Because he had been kept out of the public eye, Edward could often pass unrecognized (although the corgis might be a giveaway). Though camera-shy in his earlier days, he has now learned to accept attention as a fact of life. When, in a rag week at Cambridge, he was caught dancing on top of a bus, he knew the picture would make news. And he admitted to reporters: 'Yes, it was my idea.'

— ANNE AND MARK —

arly on the morning of 14 November 1973, an inconspicuous car took a strange, zigzag route around the back streets of London to Westminster Abbey. Inside were two young men, also inconspicuous in lounge suits. Mark Phillips, with his best man, was off to marry the only daughter of Queen Elizabeth II. The object was to avoid the crowds – and they succeeded.

Safely arrived at the Deanery, Mark and his brother officer changed into their magnificent scarlet and gold uniforms, complete with swords and spurs. 'Feeling like death,' Mark said later, 'we crept in [to the Abbey] rather like two naughty schoolboys along one of the side aisles to where we had to sit and wait.'

There were sixteen hundred wedding guests; four thousand police on duty; five military bands playing to the crowds outside; and around five hundred million pairs of eyes watching the television screen. As a fourteen-year-old American boy once observed: 'Coronations and Royal Weddings are more fun than Disneyland.'

For a shy, rather inarticulate young man it was quite an experience. Already the publicity had left him speechless and he couldn't think what to say when asked on a television interview: 'what will you say to the people you haven't asked to the wedding?' It was even harder when Prince Philip rose to propose the toast at the wedding breakfast. 'Unaccustomed as I am,' said the Prince . . . long pause . . . 'to speaking at breakfast.' He had stolen the show and everyone fell about laughing. Mark, following on, could think of little to say except 'thank you'.

In his own way, though, Mark Phillips was making royal history. It was not the first time a Prince or Princess had married a commoner. What about Princess Margaret who, only thirteen years before, had married Antony Armstrong Jones? But it was the first time that the daughter of a reigning Monarch had – with full parental approval, full pomp and circumstance – become the wife of a man so unassociated with the royal world. As a fashion photographer who had commemorated the twenty-first birthday of the Duke of Kent, taken official portraits of Prince Charles on his eighth birthday, covered any number of aristocratic marriages and been invited to dinner by any number of aristocrats, including Lady Elizabeth Cavendish who introduced him to the Princess, Tony was no stranger to grand circles. Mark Phillips was.

If there had not been the mutual interest in horses and competitive riding, would he and Anne have ever met? or become well enough acquainted to fall in love? It's like the question: would Philip and Elizabeth have made contact without their royal backgrounds? answer, probably not.

'Reminds me of my own wedding,' quipped Prince Philip as he and his daughter arrived at Westminster Abbey on 14 November 1973. And judging by the crowds and the cameras, public interest was almost as intense as on the November day, twenty-six years before, when Anne's parents were married. Neither bride nor bridegroom were demonstrative people; yet everyone could see they were radiantly in love.

Mark's family had no pretensions to rank or wealth. They had a farm in a lovely part of England and his father was a director of the Walls' food firm. Nothing royal about that. But Mark was practically brought up in the saddle and this *was* like the royals. (Queen Alexandra used to put her babies in baskets and walk them around slung over the back of a horse.) Moreover, he had great talent and determination.

He was introduced to Princess Anne, not through any aristocratic connections, but by the adjutant at Sandhurst. Mark had been a reserve member of the Olympic team which competed in Mexico. Britain had won a gold medal and Whitbreads arranged a celebration party in London. A few days before, Mark was summoned to the adjutant's office. The adjutant was 'rather a frightening chap' and 'when a little lowly cadet was summoned . . . it meant trouble, so I went there in fear and trepidation. He told me

Princess Anne was going to be a guest at the Whitbread thing, then going on for dinner afterwards, and that I was considered a suitable candidate to make up the numbers. I took a deep breath, gulped, and that was that.'

There was immediate rapport between the two – even though Mark had the embarrassment of losing one of his contact lenses as he sat beside the Princess. (He had to go back to the restaurant later and hunt for it under the table.) Thereafter they were to meet regularly – often as rivals – at horsey events. Love and marriage resulted.

Anne and Mark had been brought together by their mutual love of riding, and it has always seemed natural to see them together at horse trials – or at least with horses in the background. But although Anne says loyally that Mark copes very well with formal public engagements, he certainly looks much happier on these relaxed occasions.

There was no pressure on this Princess to produce an immediate Heir. Or if there was, she rejected it. Anne carried on riding; and when, after four years, she became pregnant, there may have been a touch of regret in her voice as she broke the news to a friend: 'Yes, I've been grounded.' Peter Phillips was born in November 1977. Zara followed in May 1981. Just before the birth of her first child, Anne was asked if she wanted a boy or a girl. She replied that, as this was the Queen's first grandchild, she supposed it ought to be a boy, '. . . but so long as it has ten fingers and ten toes, I don't really give a hoot.'

At the birth of Zara, Mark – who always said the press were waiting for him to put his foot in it – made the wrong remark. He had been present (reluctantly) at both births; and when asked by reporters what he thought about the father's participation, he commented that 'it wasn't everyone's cup of tea.' There were headlines in the *Sunday Mirror*: 'OH BABY – MARK DROPS A CLANGER!' It's now the 'in' thing for fathers to share, as far possible, the labour pains; and poor Mark was assured he had offended millions. (No such stigma attached to Prince Philip who was happily playing squash when Charles was born.)

No one could deny, however, that the Phillips' children were enchanting: perhaps the prettiest, most photogenic youngsters in the Royal Family. And there is something refreshing about their informal, no-nonsense upbringing.

It began with the names. The first child was not called a traditional George or Albert or Edward: the first two names were Peter Mark, after his Phillips grandfather and father; and the only concession to royalty was the final Andrew. Zara was called after nobody. Her parents just liked the name, and a relation said it sounded like the winner of the 3.30 at Lingfield.

Gatcombe Park is very much a family home. There are likely to be dolls on the stairs, small bicycles in the porch, fluffy toys in the drawing room. And there is no question of the children being brought down, prettily dressed by nanny, to see the parents after tea. Whenever possible, the parents will have been up in the nursery having tea all together. And whereas their uncle, little Prince Andrew, had still been put into clean clothes twice a day (all of which had to be washed and ironed by hand), Peter and Zara wear jeans and dungarees and sweaters that can be dunked in the washing machine and drip-dried. There's no constant changing of clothes. Mark and Anne don't change for dinner themselves unless it is a formal occasion.

Anne says she doubts if her children will even *feel* royal. But despite the fresh air that blows through Gatcombe, the grandchildren of the Queen can't escape the pressure of publicity. It's news when young Peter picks up a dead pheasant at a Sandringham shoot and whirls it merrily around. (Protests from the anti-blood-sporters.) Protests, too, when he's given a shiny toy pistol for Christmas and rushes around pretending to shoot Uncle Andrew and Uncle Edward. At the Queen's thirty-second wedding anniversary it's evident, world-wide, that he's disrupting the official photographs: giggling, tugging at his mother's hand and falling about on the grass. Zara, crawling around the horses at Badminton and slapped for bad behaviour by her mother, is bound to feature in the popular press. Millions are interested to know that the little Shetland pony, on which Peter and Zara have been given first riding lessons, is called Smokey.

The children look too good to be true – and that's right. There are those in the Royal Family who mutter that little Peter and Zara Phillips are allowed to run wild. And Anne is not a mother who believes her children should always be neatly dressed and impeccably behaved. But there'll be a good spanking if they go too far.

But, pressured or not, both children look lovely and happy. And as the number of young royals increases, and attention is diverted to the likely families of Prince Andrew and Prince Edward, plain Mr Peter and Miss Zara Phillips may indeed stop 'feeling royal'.

Incidentally, they are the first grandchildren of a reigning Monarch to be born without a title. If he and Princess Anne had so chosen, Mark – like Tony Armstrong Jones – could have been Lord This or Earl of the Other. The children would not then have been Miss and Master. But it was part of the normality desired by their parents. No, thank you. No title.

Peter is a purposeful looking young man, often intent on going his own way. He once disappeared in the crowds at Badminton and the alarmed detective searched and searched. He was discovered sharing an ice cream with a little girl. 'Not an easy youngster to keep track of,' commented a friend.

Peter, photographed here with his parents at Gatcombe Park, was the Queen's first grandchild.

The Queen and Anne in practical, at-the-races gear. Peter – who has been known to put out his tongue at photographers – now pretends to be shy and hides behind his hat.

Will Peter be a rider like father and mother? Almost as soon as he could toddle, he was said to be more at home in the stables than in the nursery. No coaxing was needed to get him astride the tiny Shetland pony, Smokey (now handed on to Zara). And these days, Anne assures her mother, Peter is out riding in all weather, rain or shine or snow. Another Olympic champion?

— LADY DIANA SPENCER —

BORN 1 JULY 1961, UNDER THE SIGN OF CANCER

 ancerians have one thing in common with Scorpios. Appearances can be deceptive. Not surprising – for in some ways, the Cancer girl is a bundle of contradictions. Outwardly, she is often shy and unassuming. But make no mistake: she laps up attention, thrives on publicity. She is volatile, easily hurt, given to swift tears followed by laughter. But under these April-day changes of mood, there is great tenacity. (This is the sign of the crab and crabs *hang on*.) It shows up particularly in relation to those she loves. The man who marries a Cancerian can expect many ups and downs, but she will never leave him; and if he tries to leave her, she'll fight like crazy. There's a tendency to be over-possessive with her children, even after they've grown up. This goes with a very strong maternal instinct, for, starting in childhood, the Cancer girl adores 'mothering' anything small; and if there's nothing else around, she'll mollycoddle a mouse.

Another contradiction: although vulnerable and moody, she's good at protecting herself. She retreats into her shell – the crab again – when the going gets really rough. Seems then that nothing can disturb her. Physically, she can be very glamorous. (Like Gina Lollobrigida.) And Cancerians of both sexes adore music. Witness Louis Armstrong, Richard Rogers and Ringo Starr. (Further on, we'll be looking at the Cancer man. Prince William was born under the same sign as his mother.)

The Spencer family cradle had been brought out again. It was an old-fashioned, fairy-tale affair with elaborate lace curtains and white satin ribbons dangling from the headcover. The Althorps hoped for a son, but it was hard to resent such a pretty third daughter. The old cradle was freshened up with new curtains in a pale rosebud design plus matching quilt. Here Diana slept for the first six months of her life.

Dressing up began early. On her first birthday she wore a stiff white dress with any number of ruffles and petticoats. She looked so enchanting, a friend advised

At nine Diana was getting a taste for sports and ponies. But, unluckily, a bad fall was to make her nervous of riding.

Lady Althorp to enter her for the local baby beauty contest at Sandringham; but neither father nor mother thought this a good idea.

It was a privileged upbringing – first at Park House, next door to the Queen's home at Sandringham, and later at the Spencer family seat, Althorp, in Northampton. Not many small girls are brought up so close to three royal Princes. Not every father hires a camel for his daughter's seventh birthday so that she can invite all her friends to come and play at being Lawrence of Arabia. But the word 'spoilt' was never applied to Diana. (Her nanny, Miss Thompson, remembers her as 'very sweet natured'.) Nor was she in the least pushy. Miss Ridsdale, headmistress of Diana's first boarding school, even confessed: 'I can't remember her awfully well . . . she was a perfectly nice, ordinary little girl.'

The big jolt in her young life – the separation and divorce of her parents – might well have affected her badly. The disappearance of a mother when you are only six is hard enough; but even harder perhaps was the publicity that followed. Two years later there was a bitter divorce with both parents fighting for custody of the children. Details of the case, involving of course the private life of the family, were widely reported. Diana's schoolfellows could read all about it in the papers, ask her questions, chatter behind her back.

Was this the time when Diana, true to her sign of the crab, first learned to retreat into her shell? let it all wash over her? Certainly she found a way of coping for there were no signs of her growing up maladjusted or miserable. She remained close to both parents and may even have found rewards in a double home.

Custody of the children had been given to Earl Spencer, but there were wonderful holidays in Scotland with their mother and new stepfather, Peter Shand Kydd. At home Diana was petted by her two elder sisters; and the baby of the family, Charles, was her living doll. She always adored mothering and, when nothing else was available, did indeed mollycoddle hamsters.

In later years Diana's childhood was to prove a problem for the popular press. It just wasn't spicy enough. Here was a pretty girl who enjoyed dressing up, who loved dancing and swimming, who wasn't much of a scholar, who made friends easily, who . . . what else? They had to make do with incidents like the time she was thrown, fully dressed, into a swimming pool, or when she left her Swiss finishing school after six weeks because she was homesick.

In some ways, Diana's credentials as the future Princess of Wales were almost too impeccable. For journalists, that is.

Diana as a baby, and growing up. 'A magnificent physical specimen,' her father declared. She was particularly enchanting when dressed in frilly frocks.

Diana with her brother, Charles. The affection between them is unmistakable.

— CHARLES AND DIANA —

One popular song must strike a chord with Prince Charles: 'To All the Girls I've Loved Before'. For he has never tried to conceal the fact that he fell in love easily and did so 'countless times'.

Some of his girlfriends, including Diana's own sister Sarah, were acceptable to the Royal Family. Others were a source of dismay, just as his great great grandfather's affairs had been a source of dismay to Victoria. There was much shuddering when the ex-lover of Davina Sheffield revealed that they had lived together before her association with Charles. The same thing happened with sexy Fiona Watson who, in addition, had been photographed nude in the magazine *Penthouse*. Then there was the secretary of Charles's polo club who was divorced and who prattled to the press. The list could go on and on.

But when it came to marriage, the highly susceptible Prince was cautious. 'It's the last decision,' he said, 'where I would want my heart to rule my head.' He recognized, too, that love affairs were nothing like setting up house together, having a trial run. 'It's all right for you chaps,' he told reporters in India. 'You can live with a girl before you marry her. But I can't. I've got to get it right from the word go.' Very definitely, he wanted the first wife to be the last.

Many of Charles's friends believe the choice of Diana began with the head rather than the heart. There was no question of love at first sight, for he first saw her in the nursery. When she was eight, he did give her a copy of his book, *The Old Man of Lochnager*, but much as an elder brother might have done. (At the time, he was twenty.) At the age of sixteen, she struck him as a particularly jolly girl, 'bouncy . . . full of life'. Hardly the words of a lover, even coming from an Englishman.

But he came to see that she was *very* suitable: as suitable as the brides, personally vetted by Queen Victoria, for her son and grandsons (i.e. Princess Alexandra and Princess May of Teck). Diana was descended from almost as many Kings as himself. She was familiar with the royal world, innocent of scandal, pretty and healthy. Also – and this had its effect – she was in love with him. She didn't describe him as 'bouncy' or 'jolly' but, softly, as 'pretty amazing'.

Traditionally, man is the hunter. But royals are susceptible to genuine affection. They are suspicious of being loved for their position rather than for themselves (a reason, it is suggested, that they are so fond of animals who don't know they are royal). And the fact that Diana couldn't conceal her feelings and that they were, obviously, for the man and not just the Prince . . . well, the Barbara Cartland formula was about to work. Experience (the man) was to fall for innocence (the girl).

The courtship, as everyone knows, attracted fantastic publicity. And it came hardest on the unprotected Diana. Photographers, disguised as roadsweepers, lay in wait when she left for the kindergarten in Pimlico where she worked. They even climbed into the school through the lavatory window. Fictitious stories that she and Charles had secretly met and spent the night together in the royal train circulated. And it was like the romance fever over Philip and Elizabeth: it went mad before the man had even asked 'will you marry me?'

Astonishingly, Diana could cope – keeping both her temper and her manners. 'I just don't have anything to say,' she would tell reporters. And then, disarmingly: 'I'm sorry to be so boring.'

'She gave nothing away,' said a gossip columnist. 'And she did it so nicely, so politely, you could only admire her.' (Was it the crab again? able, under pressure, to stay in the shell?)

Then the engagement was announced, and the letters and telegrams and presents poured in, and no doubt Mark Phillips was thankful he didn't have to go through all *that* again. But Diana, looking ever lovelier and ever slimmer (she lost nearly a stone before the wedding), established herself without apparent effort as the heaven-sent Princess of Wales.

On 29 July 1981, alarm clocks round the world were set for odd hours. Like 2 a.m., 3 a.m., 5 a.m. Breakfasts were postponed. Lunches were balanced on knees in front of the television set. Dinners might be forgotten. Hundreds of millions of people were determined to see Lady Diana climb into the Glass Coach and drive to St Paul's and make that long, long walk down the aisle on the unsteady arm of her half-invalid father. 'I expect to spend most of the day in tears,' said Prince Charles, for all his favourite music was played and sung and he admits this makes him cry. His eyes were certainly not dry when the hymn 'I Vow to Thee My Country' shook the dome.

At the end of the day, one doubt was expressed. It came, not from Willie Hamilton, but from a devoted royalist. She said it had been the most beautiful wedding that ever happened, '. . . but I do hope Prince Charles doesn't spend *all* his honeymoon at the wheel of the *Britannia*.'

The wedding of the decade – 29 July 1981. It was declared a public holiday in Britain.

─ MARRIED YEARS ─

I'm sorry,' said Prince Charles. 'I haven't yet found a way to cut my wife in two.'

He was talking to some disappointed members of a crowd who had hoped to meet Diana and only succeeded in meeting the Heir to the Throne. He commented, 'You've joined the wrong queue', on another occasion when the same thing happened again.

During the period leading up to the Royal Wedding, interest in Diana had reached such a peak one would think some decline was inevitable. But no. It just seemed to go on climbing to new heights. When the couple set off together on their first public engagements as Prince and Princess of Wales, one thing became clear. The person everyone *really* wanted to see and shake hands with and talk to was . . . Diana.

Charles had always wanted a wife who could handle the publicity side successfully. But he must have been taken aback by the extent of her success. He himself was hardly used to being anything but the central figure: it was like the leading man marrying a member of the chorus – and finding that the roles were beginning to be reversed.

But jealousy does not appear to be part of his make-up. Jack Kennedy once introduced himself as 'the man who accompanies Mrs Kennedy round Europe', and there was nothing but approval for his wife in the remark. However unaccustomed to losing the limelight, Charles – like Kennedy – took pleasure in the feminine appeal: 'the overwhelming effect,' as he put it, 'of my dear wife on everyone.'

Diana herself was not finding it so easy. She could play her part beautifully in public; but the total exhaustion, much suffered by Mark Phillips, was to catch up on her. A friend described her condition as '. . . flaked out . . . shattered – utterly exhausted after a public engagement. She slumps in a chair and lies there quietly without saying a word.' And it is said that this was an area where Charles was not always sympathetic. One comes back to the conditioning of royal children, to the ingrained acceptance of publicity and the work it involves. You have to go through with it; and if it turns you into a zombie off-stage, that's something you have to get over. What kind of family life would you have otherwise?

Princess Anne had decided not to rush her fences. There was no need to produce children at the first respectable moment – and many marriage counsellors would say this was sensible. Young couples, it is argued, need time to adjust to each other, to a new way of life. And

The gasp went up in the crowds: 'Oh, he kissed her!' This was on the balcony at Buckingham Palace, after the wedding. It set a new, less inhibited style – as did the kiss by the car. Royals are not usually seen embracing in public. (On her Silver Wedding Anniversary, the Queen would not even leave the church arm-in-arm with her husband.)

Two years later, a friend of Diana's was to say: 'In some ways, it's quite hard to recognize her.' The Princess was now a mother, and maybe this had helped to give her public confidence. But the great difference was in the way she had learned to live with stardom – a stardom which often eclipsed other members of the Royal Family. The eighteen-year-old who seemed to look down rather than up, who got the giggles during the national anthem, who occasionally snapped out or shed tears in public – how unlike the poised, impeccable Princess

travelling around Australia and New Zealand. 'Don't you get tired of all this?' a voice in the crowd once asked her. Diana considered the question for several moments. (It had been a specially hot, exhausting day.) Then she said: 'Not so long as he is with me', looking, of course, at Charles. The sense of a working, loving partnership stands out a mile. They seem to get strength from each other. Is this what the crowds, on Diana's first major tour overseas, found particularly beguiling? (Even more than those stunning hats and dresses!)

perhaps a waiting period is even more advisable when the new life-style is extra demanding.

But there was no real pressure on Anne to come up with an Heir. And even if Diana had not been a girl who adored babies, she, like the Queen, would probably have become pregnant very quickly. It had been expected of Queens and Princesses for centuries when Heirs to the Throne were so important; and although the present Royal Family is hardly short of sons, the old-fashioned attitude persists. Charles is the eldest. Charles ought to father the next Heir. The same old question was in the air when the Prince and Princess of Wales returned from honeymoon. Is she . . . isn't she? And if not, *why not*?

Pretty soon she was, and that was marvellous. But as Diana remarked, plaintively: 'Nobody told me about morning sickness.' Queasiness didn't help on the continuing round of public engagements – but here, at least, she could turn round on Charles and say: '*You* don't know what it's like.' And few expectant fathers could have been more concerned or gentle.

Apart from her friends and family, there were two great standbys in Diana's early married life. One, quite simply, was clothes. The other was the home at Highgrove.

She had always been interested in fashion (it ran in the family, with both her elder sisters working for *Vogue*), but it was heady stuff to discover that she could afford almost anything, and that she had the taste and the figure to win the title Leader of Fashion. She is not riotously extravagant, like Jackie Kennedy: one can't imagine her running up a bill for thousands of pounds at a department store and then assuring Charles – as Jackie assured the President – that it was just for odds and ends, a few bathing suits, some clothes for the children and so on. But Diana and Jackie do have something in common. Choosing clothes is a kind of escape hatch, a holiday from the more wearing side of their public life. And it can be justified. (Well, within reason.) Looking good *is* part of Diana's job, just as it had been part of the First Lady's. She needn't feel that this is pure self-indulgence.

Like Jackie, too, Diana loves to make a beautiful home. When Mrs Kennedy moved into the White House, she spent so much money on refurbishing that her husband declared: '. . . she's run through all the government funds . . . if the taxpayers ever found out what she's spending, they'd drive me out of office.' Again, Diana is far less lavish; but she is a perfectionist and works very hard to get things right. When the removal vans arrived at Highgrove with their huge loads of furniture, china, wedding presents and so on, Diana had

left written instructions where everything was to go. She told a friend: 'I've changed my mind six times on one room – and it's still not right.' She will spend any amount of time working on colour schemes, picking over fabrics, rearranging furniture. 'She is a very home-loving person,' said one of the staff. And added: 'She makes it clear that nothing is finished until she says it is.'

Maybe the home cannot be called 'part of the job' like the clothes. Diana is determined to keep it very private, very much a family affair. But she could say with perfect truth that anyone who spends as much time in public as she and Charles need a home they can love and enjoy.

It has been said that Diana dresses to please the men. And why not? When Ena – granddaughter of Victoria and Queen of Spain – wore a dress in this style, daring to show a leg, the Court were shocked. She had to fill the gap with an extensive petticoat. Diana gets away with it – beautifully.

Hats, glorious hats. And what wonderful things Diana has done for the 'head business'. Much credit must go to her mother, Mrs Shand Kydd, who took her newly engaged daughter to see a soft-spoken Scotsman called John Boyd. He has designed truly glorious hats for her ever since.

Another form of headdress. And tiaras, like hats, sit well on Diana. (Her hairdresser has to plan a style to suit them.)

On her Canadian tour: a Victorian style for the most modern Princess.

— ROYAL COUSINS —

It was a bumper baby year for the Royal Family – 1964. First came James Ogilvy, son of Princess Alexandra and Angus Ogilvy. Then Prince Edward, youngest son of the Queen. Then Helen Windsor, daughter of the Duke and Duchess of Kent. And, just a few days later, Sarah Armstrong Jones, daughter of Princess Margaret and Lord Snowdon.

Their birthdays were so close together that joint celebrations might be planned. When they came into their teens, there was dancing in the dungeons of Windsor Castle. The massive walls were ideal for containing the deafening pop music of the disco. And it was certainly a change from earlier days when prisoners could be locked in and left to die of hunger and thirst.

In recent years, the Royal Family have become more clannish. Prince Charles and Princess Anne had few cousins to play with; and the little Princesses, Elizabeth and Margaret, were almost isolated together. They didn't even have much contact with the sons of their aunt, George and Gerald Lascelles, although the boys were close to them in age. They came to tea occasionally, but that was all – and perhaps, in spite of the same royal background, they just didn't have enough in common. True, they all liked music; but the Princesses did not share George's deep interest in classical composers or Gerald's preference for jazz. (Young George was so serious on the subject, his grandfather George V was to observe: 'I don't understand it. His parents are perfectly normal.')

A dreamy picture of Princess Margaret and her son David, taken soon after his birth in November 1961. The photographer was Lord Snowdon. Inevitably, a picture which seems to express love, as well as skill on the part of the photographer, is sad seen in terms of later years. But the relationship between father and son has remained happy.

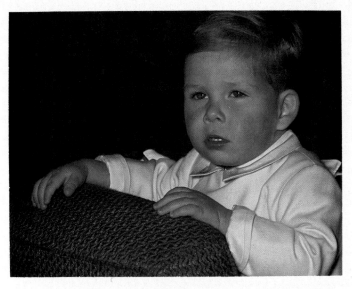

'He's just a boy whose aunt happens to be Queen,' said Princess Margaret. And young David Linley was to grow up determined to make a career independent of his royal connections.

A family group, taken by Cecil Beaton in 1964, against the background of Kensington Palace. Already one begins to see that both children have little of the Hanoverian look about them. Very definitely, they take after the father.

A typical get-together of five-year-old Prince Edward and his favourite playmate, Sarah Armstrong Jones. She was a loving and lovable child who never had trouble making friends – royal or otherwise.

Perhaps the troubles of the parents brought the children closer together. Theirs was a happy relationship, probably helping both to grow up sturdy and well-adjusted. They also remained on good terms with both father and mother.

But after Charles and Anne an increasing number of young royals were to grow up together. They shared the great Christmas celebrations at Windsor. Often they went to the same schools. James Ogilvy and George, eldest son of the Kents, were both at Eton; Helen Windsor and Marina Ogilvy went to St Mary's, Wantage; later, Helen joined Prince Edward at Gordonstoun. A second batch of young royals – three born to the Duke and Duchess of Gloucester, two to Prince and Princess Michael of Kent – live close to each other in London and make frequent contact.

One gets the impression that the young royals are very comfortable together, sharing jokes and parties and friends (like the Kennedy clan). Lord Snowdon once described the royal circle at Kensington Palace as having '. . . a language as private as a patois', and this probably applied to the children as much as to the adults. The common royal background was not enough to foster friendship between the young Princesses and the Harwoods; but the next generation discovered the truth of Prince Philip's remark: 'Children soon discover that it is safer to unburden yourself to a member of the family than just a friend.'

There are, of course, big differences between them. Some are clever: George, the eldest son of the Kents, won a scholarship to Eton, while David Linley fluffed the entrance exam. Some know what they want to do and be: Sarah Armstrong Jones has always had a special interest in design and art and, early on, set her sights on getting into the design side of theatre production. James Ogilvy, a good all-rounder, cheerfully admits that he hasn't a clue what he wants his future career to be. Some of the girls, like Helen Windsor, are dazzlingly pretty; others, like Sarah and Marina Ogilvy, rely more on charm, extrovert warmth and humour. So it's a mixed bag, but they mix well.

It's obvious that the royal rules have been much relaxed, particularly for the cousins. When you're only sixteenth or seventeenth in line for the Throne – and likely to become even further removed as Charles's family increases and Andrew's and Edward's begin – the pressure is off and freedom, undreamt of in earlier days, opens up. Queen Victoria would have found it quite unacceptable to have a nephew who chose, like David Linley, to become a commercial cabinet-maker and who was liable to appear in her presence in blue jeans with his hair full of sawdust. George V would turn in his grave at the idea of a great granddaughter, aged twenty, setting up a bachelor flat in London and entertaining a regular boyfriend without restrictions. (True of Helen Windsor.)

So what differences *are* involved in being a royal cousin today? or do they hardly exist outside the Queen's own family?

The answer is yes, differences do still exist. And they affect the children more strongly than the adults: particularly the young children who have to tread a difficult path. They are encouraged to be unsnobbish, 'just another small boy or girl'. But it's not as simple as that. Things are always cropping up which set them apart.

Some of these differences are thoroughly enjoyable. There's Christmas at Windsor. (Not at all like the Christmasses of most children.) There are invitations to glittering events, like the wedding of the Prince and Princess of Wales. Later on there'll be parties at Buckingham Place where they may meet some of the most famous people in the world: filmstars, like Paul Newman; Presidents, like Ronald Reagan; Prime Ministers, like Margaret Thatcher. (Only drawback, a young guest at Windsor once said, is that 'you don't get much to eat'. And it's true: the Queen and Prince Philip are abstemious about food and drink. Henry VIII or George IV would be

aghast to find that, for all its pomp and ceremony, a State Banquet only runs to four modest courses.)

There are special privileges for sporting events. The young Kents can sweep into Wimbledon ahead of the crowds, occupy the most enviable seats and take tea afterwards with McEnroe and Virginia Wade. No queuing either for Cup Final tickets. And when twelve-year-old Nicholas Windsor, youngest son of the Duke of Kent, attended his first match and was asked at half-time what refreshments he wanted, the brisk answer was: 'Champagne, please.'

If Sarah Armstrong Jones wants to attend the *première* of the latest, most heavily booked play or musical, that's not likely to be a problem. And even when her brother, David, is flying tourist class, he will be welcome in any VIP lounge. Although their parents insist that they are just children who happen to have an aunt/grandmother/near cousin as Queen (even Princess Margaret, who has a strong sense of her own position, takes this view), the privileges don't go away. Neither do the pressures.

Children dislike too much watching and following; and in the outside world, the young royals have to live with the careful, restrictive eye of a detective. Coming home from school Peter Phillips often begs to be allowed to play on the swings in the public park. Usually the detective says 'no'; it would attract too much attention.

The 'Presence', as he is sometimes called, can become even more aggravating later on. A girlfriend of Prince Andrew once described him as '. . . the biggest passion killer in the business'.

'All this happened to me,' said the Duchess of Gloucester, *'just by falling in love.'* By *'all this'* she meant the royal connection. When the Danish girl, Birgitte Eva Van Deurs, met Richard of Gloucester at a Cambridge tea party, she didn't even know he was a Prince. When that registered, she never expected to be Duchess, for Richard was the second son.

But six weeks after their wedding in 1972, the elder brother, William, was killed in an air race. The Duke and Duchess accept their Royal Family responsibilities, but like to create their own style. Perhaps this shows up in the choice of their children's clothes: not the conventional upper-class togs, but – as you can see – an Edwardian, sometimes Victorian look. Note the long pink coat and snazzy white handbag of little Lady Rose. (Very unlike the informal, country-gentry look of the Phillips family and the Ogilvies.)

Lady Davina Windsor, the second child.

Lady Rose Windsor, the youngest.

Alexander, Earl of Ulster, the eldest.

The watch-your-step, watch-your-tongue rule still applies. It may not be as acute as the caution impressed on the young Charles, but the fact remains: almost anything they do or say just might be splashed out across the national newspapers.

Public interest extends to trivia. A nurserymaid, long retired from Buckingham Palace, once complained that to this day people pestered her with questions like: Did Prince Andrew like Rice Crispies better than Sugar Puffs?' (As a matter of fact, he didn't much like either.) Friends of the young royals make the same complaint. A Bedales

The Duke and Duchess of Kent have three children: George, Earl of St Andrew's, born in 1962; Lady Helen Windsor, born in 1964; and Lord Nicholas Windsor, born in 1970.

schoolfellow of Sarah said: 'Why is it important to know when she started to use eye shadow? The press seem to think it *matters*.' Marina Ogilvy objects to being quizzed about her hobbies and talents. All right – she likes acting and swimming and playing the piano. So do millions of other girls.

The young royals must also suffer from the spotlight which, on occasions, picks out their parents. The very young can be protected: little Zara Phillips is hardly likely to register reports that her parents' marriage is shaky because their father stayed on the farm while their mother went to spend her birthday at Balmoral. The baby Gabriella was not concerned when the press reported a royal row between her mother, Princess Michael, and the Queen. (It was about the rooms allocated to the Kent family at Windsor over Christmas.)

But some publicity is far more painful. James was twelve and Marina ten when 'the Lonrho affair' blew up in 1976. The company was accused of defying British sanctions against Rhodesia; and although Angus Ogilvy had resigned from Lonrho three years earlier, he was still involved in the criticisms and came in for a lot of public stick. There might have been some publicity, even if he'd married a Miss Jones instead of Princess Alexandra; but almost certainly it wouldn't have been on the same scale. Unlikely, too, that he would have felt it necessary to resign from all his other directorships. It's bad enough for a family when such things happen; but far worse when the children – and their friends – are going to read all about it in the papers.

Even worse for the children was the enormous coverage given to the break-up of the Snowdon marriage, to the instability of their mother (she was reported to suffer from suicidal depression and to be on the verge of alcoholism), and to her association with a man seventeen years younger than herself, Roddy Llewellyn. There were blunt suggestions, too, that the Princess was 'not doing her job', should forego her income from the taxpayer and retire from public life.

But this was an occasion when a comment on family life by Princess Anne rang true. 'The greatest advantage of my life is the family I grew up in. The family was always there, the feeling of being in a family, and we were the stronger for it.' Certainly the royal ranks closed to protect Princess Margaret and her children – especially Sarah who was the youngest and the most vulnerable. The Queen practically adopted her as a second daughter. 'Whenever Sarah was at Sandringham or Windsor,' said a member of the Royal Household, 'she followed the Queen around like a shadow. It was much closer than the usual aunt and niece relationship. I think the Queen felt she needed extra love and attention, and she always found time to give it.'

The out-of-the-ordinariness for the royal cousins exists; but the British knack for compromise, for moving with the times, is much in evidence. When Princess Alexandra, the Duke of Kent, the Duchess of Gloucester and Princess Anne say they want their children to have a normal upbringing . . . to be treated like any other children . . . it may not be quite practical. But the wish is genuine and genuine steps are taken to make it as true as possible.

There are no special privileges for the children at school. They eat the same food, make their own beds, muck in on the same chores as anyone else. They're not even excused for special occasions. Marina Ogilvy was not allowed to attend the Queen Mother's eightieth birthday celebrations because she was in the middle of revising for her O-levels.

Schools are chosen because they are relaxed and sensible rather than starchy and snobby. Bedales, chosen for the Snowdon children, is notoriously easy-going. It allows children to develop their own talents; and David Linley, who is no great academic, was encouraged to follow his undoubted flair for woodwork. There's no school uniform and even punk hair-styles are tolerated. It's co-ed, only stipulating that the boys and girls must sleep apart in two dormitories: one known as Boys' Flat, the other as Girls' Flat. At this stage, Sarah was something of a tomboy and enjoyed playing with the male brigade. It could hardly be more unlike the isolated schoolroom of their mother – and Margaret must have thought this was a good idea.

St Mary's Wantage is run by Anglican nuns and, as one might expect, is more formal. But it's no great respecter of rank or wealth. 'You might never realize that the girl in the bed next to yours owned half of Scotland,

Children near – but not too near – to the Throne, like Lady Helen Windsor, are sometimes said to have the best of all worlds. They can have a relaxed childhood, eating iced lollies like other youngsters, and also enviable invitations to the most exciting royal events.

The Duke of Kent was a lieutenant in the Scots Greys when he met Katharine Worsley. He was very serious about his army career, which included active service abroad. (He is seen here with his wife and eldest son in Hong Kong.) In June 1976, he had risen to the rank of Lieutenant-Colonel; but then he decided to take up the post of Vice-Chairman of the British Overseas Trade Board. He felt he could do more for his country that way. Wimbledon, he says, 'is icing on the cake'. Earning his daily bread is more important.

commented one pupil. And the royal connections of Helen Windsor and Marina Ogilvy never emerged as a barrier between them and the others.

Earlier royals had not exactly been protected when they mixed with young people of their own age. Prince Bertie, later George VI, had indeed been much bullied as a naval cadet at Dartmouth. He was teased about his knock knees and stick-out ears. (His nickname was Bat Lugs.) Boys pricked him with pins to see if his blood was really blue. But the royal 'apartness' had to be a fact of his life. Royal children might be exposed to the outside world, but they were *not* encouraged to make friends in it.

Today, David Linley will probably be settling down in a converted Dorking Bakery – his workshop – to a lunch of fish fingers with his colleague and flatmate, Charlie Wheeler-Carmichael. Everyone, including the delivery men, calls him David. He doesn't object to his title, Viscount Linley: '. . . it just isn't necessary for what I'm doing at this stage.' He has progressed from the first public display of his wares: a sycamore bowl, a towel rack and a toilet-roll holder exhibited at Parnham House, a small woodcraft school which he attended after Bedales. Now he and Charlie will be working on more ambitious projects: oak chests, rainbow screens, rosewood boxes, glass and sycamore dining tables. Some of their products will be sold for hundreds, if not thousands, of pounds.

His sister, Sarah, won a coveted place at the Camberwell School of Art. It is truly believed that there was no question of royal favouritism (unlike the case of her great uncle, the Duke of Gloucester, who was accepted at Eton even though a pretty good dunce at his lessons): she succeeded on merit. At the moment she is on a sabbatical and is working in the East End of London as an assistant to film producer Richard Godwin.

Helen Windsor is working at an art gallery in London. In due course her two brothers and her two Ogilvy cousins will find themselves a job. The Duke of Kent has gone on record as saying that members of the Royal Family must, one way or another, find ways to earn their daily bread. There's no question of the young royal cousins sitting around, waiting to get married or feeling that the grateful government owes them a living. They'll be out working like anyone else.

The privileges – and, more agreeably, the pressures – of royalty can be phased out as they grow older. (Who would recognize Gerald Lascelles as first cousin of the Queen if he walked into the room? Who knows, or particularly cares, that he married someone called Angela Dowding and has a son called Henry?) The children of the Monarch have the title Royal Highness and are expected to take on public engagements. The children of the Monarch's sons have the same title and the same

The face of Princess Alexandra is very well known. But quite possibly her two children – James Robert Bruce, born in 1964, and Marina Victoria Alexandra, born in 1966 – might pass unnoticed in a crowd.

obligations. This applies to Princess Alexandra, the Duke of Kent and Prince Michael, children of George V's son, George. Also to Richard, Duke of Gloucester, child of George V's third son, Henry.

Thereafter, the Royal Highness dies out. James and Marina Ogilvy; George, Helen and Nicholas, children of the Duke of Kent; Alexander, Davina and Rose, children of the Duke of Gloucester; Frederick and Gabriella, children of Prince Michael – none of them is a Royal Highness or expected to take on public engagements. Neither are the Snowdon or Phillips children, because the title only passes through the son of a Monarch, not a daughter (like Princess Margaret or Princess Anne).

The new generation of royal cousins may stay part of the royal clan. But this is a matter of choice. If, like Gerald Lascelles, they decide to fade out, the Queen is not going to crack a whip and get them back in line. And there is a difference here between the royal clan and the Kennedy clan.

There might be special burdens placed on an eldest Kennedy son. But *all* Kennedys were expected to live up to the standards imposed by the formidable heads of the dynasty, Joseph and Rose. The third generation, every one

of them, were conditioned to feel '. . . that they had a destiny to fulfil. From the time they had been small enough to scrape their knees at play they had been taught that Kennedys didn't cry. Kennedys were different.' It was never good enough for a Kennedy, any Kennedy, to come second in a competition – even an egg-and-spoon race. If they weren't first, they were a bit of a disgrace.

The royal clan are not blanketed with the same expectations. One comes back to the Duke of Kent's rule of thumb: they must be able to earn their own livings. Could be as a photographer, a soldier, a carpenter, an architect, a bigwig in ICI or an illustrator of children's books. They don't have to come first. They just have to do it as well as they can. (But he would probably draw the line at gossip columnists or striptease artists.)

Princess Michael with daughter, Lady Gabriella, born in 1981. A son, Lord Frederick, had been born in 1979 and his mother observed, admiringly: 'What large hands he has – he'll make a marvellous plumber.' Like the Gloucesters, Princess Michael sets her own style, dressing her children in distinctively Austrian clothes. All these royal cousins have been described as being 'on the edge of family pictures'. Perhaps this is one way to make them stand out and assert their own characters.

PRINCE WILLIAM

The Cancer boy is not altogether easy: restless, inquisitive, emotional and – quite often – jealous of younger brothers or sisters who may hog some of the attention which, he feels, ought to be his. The umbilical cord is slow to dissolve: he adores his mother and will resent a father who takes up too much of her time. Best thing to do when he's upset is send him swimming. He's a natural water baby with a passion for the seashore. Splashing in the waves, playing in the sand will keep him happy almost indefinitely.

Parents must accept the fact that he is easily hurt, will weep buckets if slighted, and needs extra dollops of love and sympathy. They must also watch his food intake. Cancer boys adore eating, particularly sweets, though – emotional again – they can starve themselves when life is demanding. Nickname at school is likely to be either Fatty or Skinny. (Henry VIII and the Duke of Windsor were both Cancerians.)

As an adult, he will retain very vivid memories of his childhood and, like his eating habits, they will run to extremes. Either all sunshine and happiness or all gloom and doom. A difficult childhood can warp his life. (Perhaps a clue to the problems of the Duke of Windsor?) And parents must take his moods of despair seriously. He's not putting on an act: it's for real. Bullying at school is more of a disaster for him than for most. There's a story of a Cancerian who saved up all his pocket money one term, not even indulging in his favourite sweets. When asked what it was for, he said: 'To give the boy who was nicest to me.'

They can shrivel within their crab shell and achieve very little. Or they can turn out dynamite, like Julius Caesar and John D. Rockefeller, and brilliantly creative, like Rembrandt and Ernest Hemingway.

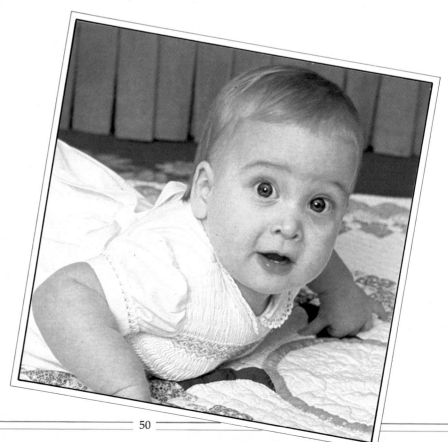

Prince William – the baby who is undoubtedly centre stage. His mother's colour sense is evident in the nursery quilt beneath him – an attractive patchwork in pale blues and greens.

Doting mother and baby, showing very clearly that Diana
does not share Victoria's view that 'an ugly baby is a very
nastly object and even the prettiest is frightful when
undressed'. William was not, in fact, as photogenic as some of
his cousins. (Most photogenic of all are the Phillips' children.)
But he can be seen as 'a little character' very early on.

There was no need for fertility experts to rally round with moonstones or recipes of sage and wood ash. A month after the honeymoon, Diana was pregnant; and in spite of morning sickness, which came as such a disagreeable surprise, everything went well. She was, as her gynaecologist George Pinker, observed '. . . a particularly healthy young woman'.

The Queen's own children had all been born in Buckingham Palace. But Princess Anne, and then Princess Michael, had decided to put themselves in the care of St Mary's, Paddington. 'It's like the dentist,' Anne is reported to have said. 'You want to go where the equipment is.' Diana followed their example.

Earlier royal babies had arrived at inconvenient moments, giving rise to much confusion. The first son of Edward VII and Alexandra was premature and the labour pains began when the mother was watching an ice hockey match at Windsor. All arrangements for the birth had been made at Marlborough House in London, but there simply wasn't time to get there. Alexandra was hustled to the unprepared Windsor Castle, an SOS went out for the local doctor, and the Lady-in-Waiting, Lady Macclesfield, was obliged to act as midwife. (Luckily, she had had thirteen children of her own and knew the form.) As all baby clothes were lacking, she tore up one of her petticoats to wrap up the tiny Prince who weighed less than 4 pounds.

The birth of Prince William caused no such dramas. He gave notice of his impending arrival when Diana was in London: she was whisked, as planned, into the private room set aside for her at St Mary's. He was born the evening of the same day, weighing a healthy 7 pounds 1½ ounces. Charles remained, devotedly, at his wife's bedside; and if, like Mark Phillips, he felt the father's participating role was 'not everyone's cup of tea', he was far too canny a hand with the press to admit it. He told the crowds the baby was 'beautiful' and 'in marvellous form'. Twenty-four hours later when Diana – setting a royal precedent – insisted on going home, Charles lovingly helped to carry the baby.

William's first journey home.
His first plane journey (right) to and from Balmoral
set a precedent, for traditionally royal parents and
their children did not travel in the same plane. Diana
overruled this law.

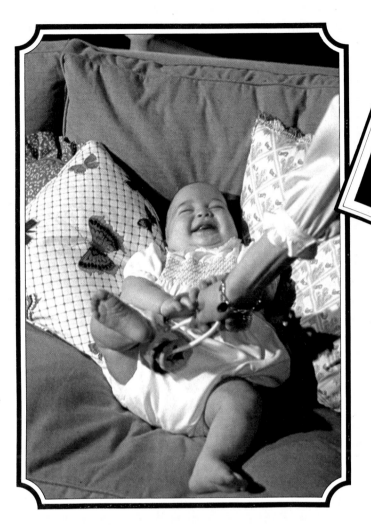

No question of the little
Prince being pushed in his
pram round St James's Park
— as was possible with his
father. Barbara and baby are
far too well known and
would attract too many
crowds.

William did not smile all that readily. It needed his
mother's hand, just seen here in the background
tickling his stomach, to get this undeniably cuddly
baby beaming.

A new style of nanny: not the rather formidable-
looking Nurse Lightbody in uniform, but a young,
attractive girl who likes to be known as Barbara.

There was no question of an unfinished nursery and sleeping in the father's dressing room (as had been the case with Princess Anne). Everything was in perfect order, including a delightful room decorated with red, white and blue rabbits. Baby gifts, which had been pouring in from all over the world, were tidily stacked away for future use. There were the usual bibs and bootees and shawls; but Charles and Diana were particularly impressed by a book of nursery rhymes made entirely in lace. It was exquisite, representing no less than ten thousand working hours by lace-makers in a Devonshire village called Beer.

The chosen nanny, Barbara Barnes, was also in readiness. She had had no formal training in her career – no course with Norland Nannies – but Charles and Diana were more inclined to trust the word of their old friends, Colin and Anne Tennant. Barbara had looked after their

children and they said she had had just the right mixture of gentleness, firmness and common sense. The children loved her, but she knew how to make them behave. She sounded just right for the future William V.

Astrological advice given to parents of Cancer children – i.e. extra dollops of love and attention – was to prove unnecessary. Queen Victoria might say: 'An ugly baby is a very nasty object and the prettiest is frightful when undressed.' But the parents of young William were immediately blind with love. He was not, in fact, a particularly pretty baby. Rounded and sturdy, yes; but a bit moon-faced and crabby-looking.

Predictably, Diana – the great baby-lover – thought he was gorgeous. But Charles was even more besotted, busily detecting smiles when there were, realistically, no more than windy grimaces. Playtime and bathtime were

cherished occasions for the father as well as the mother. He was just as appalled as Diana at the thought of leaving William behind on their travels.

The christening, as mentioned earlier, took place in the Music Room at Buckingham Palace. On 4 August 1982 he was named William Arthur Philip Louis by the Archbishop of Canterbury; and six godparents renounced the world, the flesh and the Devil on his behalf. Four of the godparents – Princess Alexandra, ex-King Constantine of Greece, Lord Romsey and the Duchess of Westminster – were fairly conventional. But the writer Laurens van der Post and the Lady-in-Waiting Susan Hussey, were less predictable. They seemed to be a very personal and affectionate choice: a luxury which Princes and Princesses of Wales have seldom indulged. 'I'm very fond of both of them' was the only reason Susan Hussey gave when asked why she had been picked as godmother by Charles and Diana.

William's christening was a joint celebration. On the same day, the Queen Mother blew out eighty-two candles on her birthday cake and attended a stunning performance of *The Pirates of Penzance* at Drury Lane. Meanwhile, her great grandson retired from the splendours of the Music Room and the flashing of the camera to the peace of his red, white and blue rabbits, and to the ministrations of Barbara Barnes. (She liked to be called Barbara and not Nanny.) We don't know if he went on crying, but its certain he wouldn't be pacified by a dummy. As Diana was to say later: 'He's never had a dummy. He has to make do with his thumb.'

William at his christening (left), with godparents ex-King Constantine of Greece, Princess Alexandra, Lord Romsey, the Duchess of Westminster, the Lady Susan Hussey and Sir Laurens Van der Post. Another picture of mother and baby (below) which says, louder than words: 'Isn't he scrumptious? I could play with him all day.'

WILLIAM'S FIRST TWO YEARS ———

He had been exposed to a fascinated public at the christening. Stories were printed of how his grandmother and great grandmother tried, without success, to stop his cries; and the photograph of Diana, who eventually succeeded by the simple expedient of putting her finger in his mouth, appeared in newspapers and magazines round the world.

Thereafter, William retreated from the public eye for some months. The royal nanny had still found it possible to push the baby Charles around St James's Park without attracting too much attention – even though the old, heavy pram stuck out as a curiousity. Nurse Lightbody was said 'to trundle it like an artillery piece'. But there was no question of walks in public places for William. The press would have been swarming like bees. So the baby was pushed around the carefully guarded gardens of Highgrove House – which are big – or taken into the private garden of Kensington Palace – which is small.

If the press wanted stories about him, they had to invent them. The parents let it be known that he was growing well and, yes, he did like his teddy bear. But the royal staff, and particularly Barbara Barnes and the under-nanny Olga Powell, were models of discretion. In early days, members of the Royal Household talked freely to outsiders, happily discussing the details of the Queen's latest miscarriage or the whippings of the Princes. But nowadays, only members of the press office are allowed to give (carefully controlled) information to the public. The Royal Household is under strict orders to say nothing. When Peter Phillips arrived for his first day at a nursery school, a reporter noticed a bump on his head. He asked the nanny what had caused it. 'No comment!' she snapped – though it was discovered later that the reason was hardly dramatic. He had tumbled off his bicycle the day before.

A story was, however, about to break. In the spring of 1983, Charles and Diana were scheduled to visit Australia and New Zealand and it was announced that William would go, too.

Not a big story, you might think, but it set a royal precedent. When George VI and Queen Elizabeth went on a nine-month journey round the world, there was no question of taking their first baby daughter with them. Little Charles and Anne stayed home whenever the Queen and Prince Philip travelled abroad. So William was the first royal baby to be included on an official visit. There may have been some arguments about it, but even this seems unlikely. Diana was determined. Charles, the doting father, supported her. And both the Queen and the Queen Mother, remembering the trauma of leaving their own babies for long spells, would have found it difficult to disagree.

The decision brought William back into the limelight. The press couldn't penetrate Highgrove House or Kensington Palace, but on a goodwill tour of the Commonwealth, it would be impossible to keep the little Prince shut away. So, even before the plane took off, there was some relaxation. William, aged six months, was photographed in a blue-and-white set of rompers with puffed sleeves. Some of the fashion pundits called it 'old fashioned', but replicas started selling like hot cakes. When he appeared in embroidered romper suits, demand was so great that a children's clothing firm in Derbyshire – which had been closed for seventeen months – re-opened to turn them out. William had helped to bring down unemployment.

The Prince performed rather solemnly in Australia. Carried out into the dazzling sunshine, and a bit disconcerted by a fly which immediately settled on his head, he refused to smile on his first appearance. But nobody minded. The people were almost as intrigued by the new baby as they were by the new Princess. They were enchanted to hear that Diana would gladly swop places with an Australian housewife who had to look after her bawling baby all the time and could never park him with a nanny. They laughed at Charles's quip: 'We're bringing him up on kangaroo meat.' They were pleased to hear that, equipped with water wings, William was taking his first swim in the pool at Woomargama, his base in New South Wales, and that, according to his father, 'his great interest is now wastepaper baskets',

He continued solemn in New Zealand. 'We tried everything to get a smile out of him,' said a lady who worked in his quarters. 'He just looked very seriously down at us from beneath the banisters on the landing, as if to remind us of our place.'

Physically, William does not bear much resemblance to the other Cancerian, his great great uncle the Duke of Windsor. But a friend of the Duke's remembers: 'He didn't smile often. Most of the time he looked very serious. But when he *did* smile, it was dazzling.'

William on his first public engagements abroad in Australia and New Zealand, proudly shown off by his parents. Certainly a far cry from the day when royal babies would be dumped, almost immediately, with wet nurses and foster parents while the King and Queen travelled on. Poor King John was abandoned little more than a year after his birth in 1167 to a very austere French monastery. He did not return to England until he was six years old.

At eighteen months old, William had his first walking session with photographers. He had been a bit slow to crawl, and not a precocious toddler. But the time had come when he could stand on his own two feet and a photographic session was arranged in the small garden of Kensington Palace.

William, dressed in a navy blue jump suit, was brought out by his parents and urged, '. . . show them how you can walk.' The Prince, faced with thirty strangers and thirty cameras, immediately headed in the opposite direction. 'Come here, Wills,' said his father, bringing him back. But William went his own way twice before facing up to his responsibilities. 'You know,' said one of the photographers later, 'he suddenly reminded me so much of old Queen Mary. That determined jowl . . .'

But the smile did come. 'Who's that?' said Diana, pointing to Charles. And suddenly a beam spread right across the small face. '*Daddy.*' (Royal children usually call their fathers 'Papa', but William seems to have adopted the name used by Diana for her own father.)

A friend once said: 'You often don't know what Diana is thinking. She hides behind her smiles.' William, one suspects, will never hide behind smiles. His protection is more likely to be the grave Hanoverian expression, the steady Hanoverian eyes. But if he's true to the Cancer sign, there'll be a lot going on underneath. And some of it may be very emotional and very surprising.

It is impossible to guess how many children, all over the world, started to be dressed in appliquéd jackets and navy blue. Certainly there was a great run on one of William's early white romper suits – even though white is hardly a practical colour for young children. We haven't seen his water gear yet, but the Princess admits he has a passion for swimming – and it's only a matter of time before William-style water-wings make the fashion news.

William takes to the cameras. At one time he had been inclined to turn his back on them; but then, quite suddenly, they became intriguing objects which he wanted to inspect. This is like his father. Photographer John Scott remembers that the little Charles always wanted to get inside the cameras and help to load and unload the film. ('He was precocious, too. When he was hardly three years old he could pronounce my Yugoslavian name, Colonel Voynovich, as well as if he'd been brought up in Belgrade!') We don't know yet how clever William is going to be, but the picture is certainly one of a sturdy, inquisitive, self-possessed youngster. How he will react to Number Two baby in his family is perhaps the question most people will want to have answered.

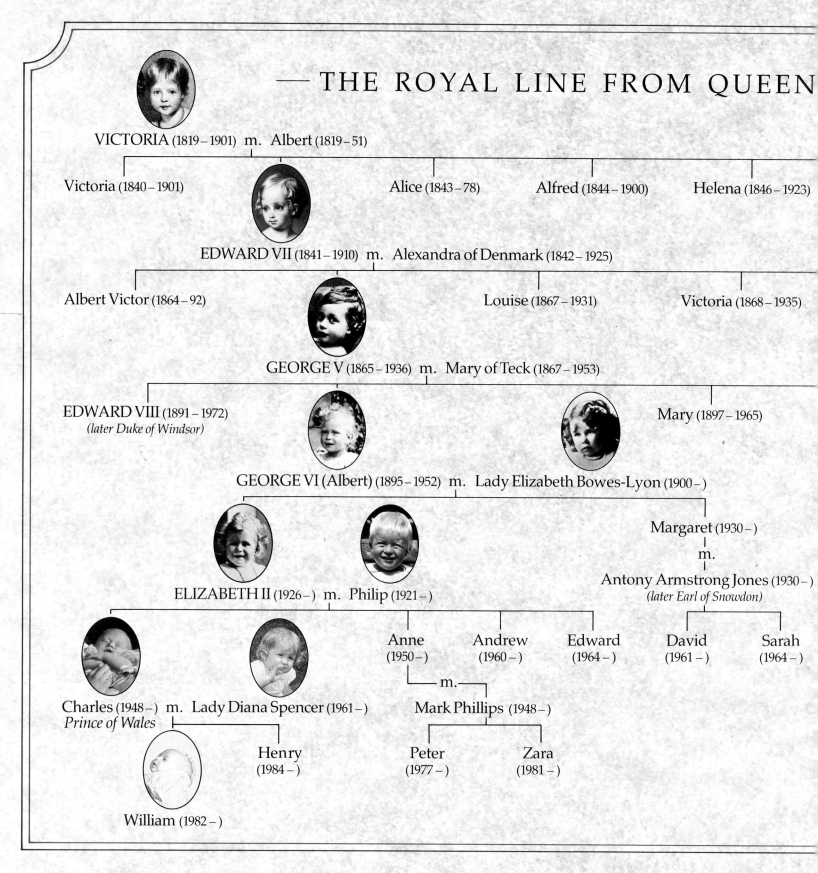

VICTORIA (1819–1901) m. Albert (1819–51)

Victoria (1840–1901)   Alice (1843–78)   Alfred (1844–1900)   Helena (1846–1923)

EDWARD VII (1841–1910) m. Alexandra of Denmark (1842–1925)

Albert Victor (1864–92)   Louise (1867–1931)   Victoria (1868–1935)

GEORGE V (1865–1936) m. Mary of Teck (1867–1953)

EDWARD VIII (1891–1972)
(later Duke of Windsor)   Mary (1897–1965)

GEORGE VI (Albert) (1895–1952) m. Lady Elizabeth Bowes-Lyon (1900–)

Margaret (1930–)

m.

Antony Armstrong Jones (1930–)
(later Earl of Snowdon)

ELIZABETH II (1926–) m. Philip (1921–)

Anne
(1950–)   Andrew
(1960–)   Edward
(1964–)   David
(1961–)   Sarah
(1964–)

m.

Charles (1948–) m. Lady Diana Spencer (1961–)
Prince of Wales

Mark Phillips (1948–)

Henry
(1984–)

Peter
(1977–)   Zara
(1981–)

William (1982–)

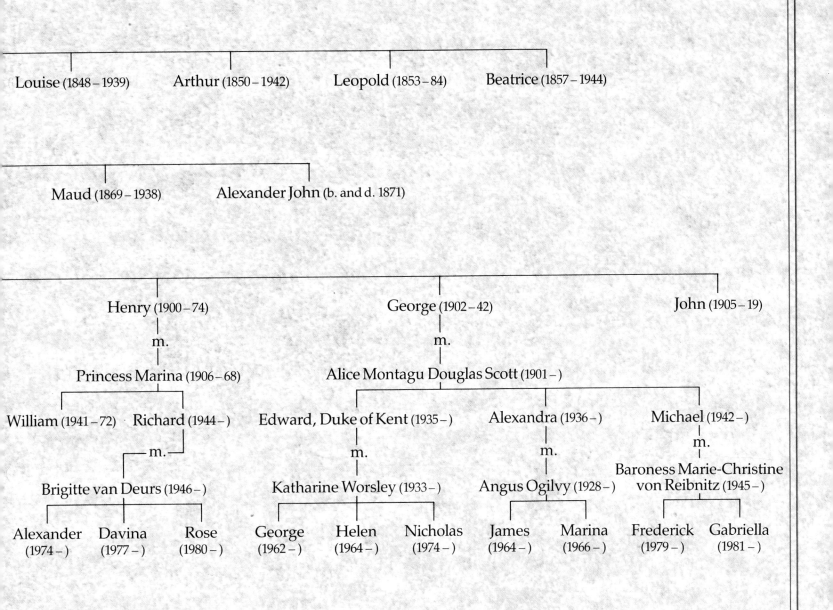

Louise (1848 – 1939) Arthur (1850 – 1942) Leopold (1853 – 84) Beatrice (1857 – 1944)

Maud (1869 – 1938) Alexander John (b. and d. 1871)

Henry (1900 – 74) George (1902 – 42) John (1905 – 19)

m. m.

Princess Marina (1906 – 68) Alice Montagu Douglas Scott (1901 –)

William (1941 – 72) Richard (1944 –) Edward, Duke of Kent (1935 –) Alexandra (1936 –) Michael (1942 –)

m. m. m. m.

Brigitte van Deurs (1946 –) Katharine Worsley (1933 –) Angus Ogilvy (1928 –) Baroness Marie-Christine von Reibnitz (1945 –)

Alexander (1974 –) Davina (1977 –) Rose (1980 –) George (1962 –) Helen (1964 –) Nicholas (1974 –) James (1964 –) Marina (1966 –) Frederick (1979 –) Gabriella (1981 –)

— PRINCE HARRY —

BORN 15 SEPTEMBER 1984, UNDER THE SIGN OF VIRGO

illiam had better watch out. Virgos can be lovely, talented, successful people: as, for example, Maurice Chevalier, Agatha Christie, Leonard Bernstein and Sophia Loren. But they can be awkward customers: cool, nit-picking, stingy, and remarkably good at getting their own way – yes, even when they *are* Number Two to a future King. There's often a ruthless streak, well illustrated by Joseph Kennedy; and emotional up-and-downers, like William and Diana, may find them strange and steely. Prince Harry can expect a long life: Virgos fuss about their health but keep going for ages. Like Prince Albert, he will probably make a faithful rather than a fiery lover, and, like Elizabeth I, he will probably be able to control inconvenient passions. No question of *him* giving up the Crown for the woman he loves. Seems a bit unfair, but the cool controlled Virgo is immensely attractive to the opposite sex. Maybe they look on him as a challenge!

Royal births, like royal weddings, present a problem to republicans. If the Monarchy is out-dated, extravagant and undemocratic, how come this upsurge of interest when Prince Harry is born? and not only interest, sheer *happiness?* When the birth was announced to the crowds outside St Mary's, Paddington, the cries of delight so startled a passing motorist, he drove slap into the side of an ambulance.

For two days, local shopkeepers had been doing a brisk trade in ladders. Photographers from all over the world were climbing everywhere to get those first shots. Diana going into the hospital, hand-in-hand with her husband. Charles coming out to tell his well-wishers '. . . he's a marvellous baby. . . eyes a sort of pale blue . . . hair an indeterminate colour. . . we'll soon have a complete polo team.' Then there were shots of young William, staggering up the steps to meet his new brother. And, of course, the Princess herself, emerging with her second precious bundle.

There was no question of Princess Diana keeping out of the public eye while pregnant. She was seen around many times, always looking slim.

Even at Odstock (right), her last public engagement before the birth, the baby is almost invisible. She and Prince Charles were visiting a centre for handicapped young people.

A great moment coming up for Prince William. Father and son going into St Mary's Hospital for the first meeting with new brother Harry.

There was practically nothing the world didn't want to know about the occasion. They were interested to hear that the baby had been born in a room only 12 feet square with linoleum on the floor. It was certainly a contrast to the labour of Jane Seymour, wife of another famous Henry. She lay propped up on velvet crimson cushions, surrounded by arcadian scenes newly painted on the walls of her great chamber.

But although there was nothing grand about the first surroundings of Prince Harry, concern for the new royal baby was just as intense as it had been for the son of Henry VIII, all those hundreds of years ago. White bootees arrived by balloon. The children in the hospital all signed a card of good wishes to Princess Diana. Flowers flooded in. Earl Spencer, the anxious grandfather, admitted: 'I sat by the telephone all day.' A member of the crowd said: 'You don't really know why you enjoy it so much. It's like enjoying cricket or the Beatles or ice-cream. You just do.'

There *were* criticisms; but they didn't have much to do with views on the Monarchy. There were those who muttered that Diana was wrong to leave hospital so soon after the birth. It might be setting a bad example to mothers who were less young and healthy. And what about Prince Charles dashing off to play polo, only an hour after his wife and the new baby had returned home? Up to then, it was acknowledged, he had behaved impeccably. He had stayed by her side all through the nine hours of labour: holding her hand, rubbing her back, mopping her brow. Shouldn't he have stayed put at Kensington Palace, at least for the first day?

But even here, he had his defenders. As one put it: 'He needed a break. And it's not as if he could feed the baby.'

The euphoria subsides, but the interest remains. The public will want to hear about Prince Harry's presents. (The first, incidentally, was given in July by the singer, Barry Manilow. It's an antique baby piano, just five inches high, which had been specially restored in New York.) They'll want

Everyone hoped to see a little bit more of the new baby, but it was a damp day and, like a careful mother, the Princess had wrapped up little Harry very thoroughly.

Leaving the hospital with a confident wave to the press. Charles said his two sons got along beautifully, right from the first moment.

to know how the relationship between the two little brothers develops. Will there be the closeness, the affection that existed between Eddy and George, the two sons of Edward VII?; the biting and kicking of Elizabeth and Margaret?; may William even be as jealous as one small boy who, when told that his new brother had 'flown in through the window,' bawled: 'well give him back his wings so he can fly out again!' The first meetings between William and Harry are reported to have been a great success. 'William keeps getting into the cot with

him and cuddling him,' Charles has reported. Grandfather Spencer thinks it will do the elder boy all the good in the world 'to have someone to fight with.'

And what of the future? perhaps future Princes and Princesses? All we know for sure is that the public will be following the royal story every step of the way. For perhaps, when all is said and done, this is the nicest thing about royal babies. There's all the interest of the here and now, and the promise of so much more to come.

The first, and probably the last, showing of Henry Charles Albert David – until he faces the cameras at his christening.

The gesture that says it all: we're so happy for you, Princess Diana. For you and your lovely new baby.

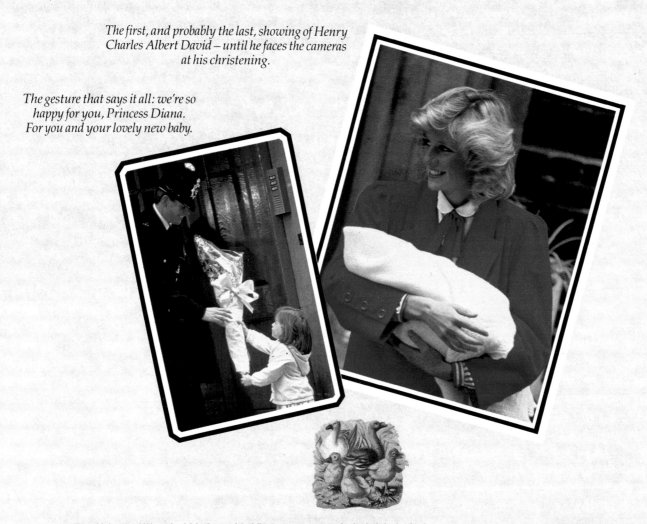

The publishers would like to thank John Scott and the following organizations and individuals for their kind permission to reproduce the photographs on the pages listed below:

BBC Hulton Picture Library 2 left, 13 below centre; Camera Press Ltd 1, 3, 5, 6, 8, 9 above left and above centre, 10-11, 12, 14 below right, 15, 19, 21 above left, 23 below left, 27 right, 30-31, 32, 33, 38 below, 39 above right, 40, 41 above and below left, 42, 43 above right, 45 above left, 46, 48 left, 49, 51, 52, 53 above left and below right, 55, 56 above, 58 left, 62 left and centre, 63 right and left, 64 right; Tim Graham 50; The Photo Source/Keystone 4 right, 7, 9 above and centre right and below left, 11 left and below right, 14 above and below right, 16 left, 18, 28 above right; Photographers International Ltd/Jayne Fincher 44, 45 below left; Popperfoto 4 left; Press Association 34, 35, 54; Rex Features 53 above right, 62 right, 64 left; Royal Archives Windsor Castle 13 above right; John Shelley 39 above and below left and below right, 41 below right, 56 below, 57, 58 right, 59; Topham 11 above right; all the other photographs by John Scott.

The publishers would also like to thank Theo Bergstrom whose special photography appears on pages 10-11, 30-31, 36-37.